THE SUPERCARRIERS

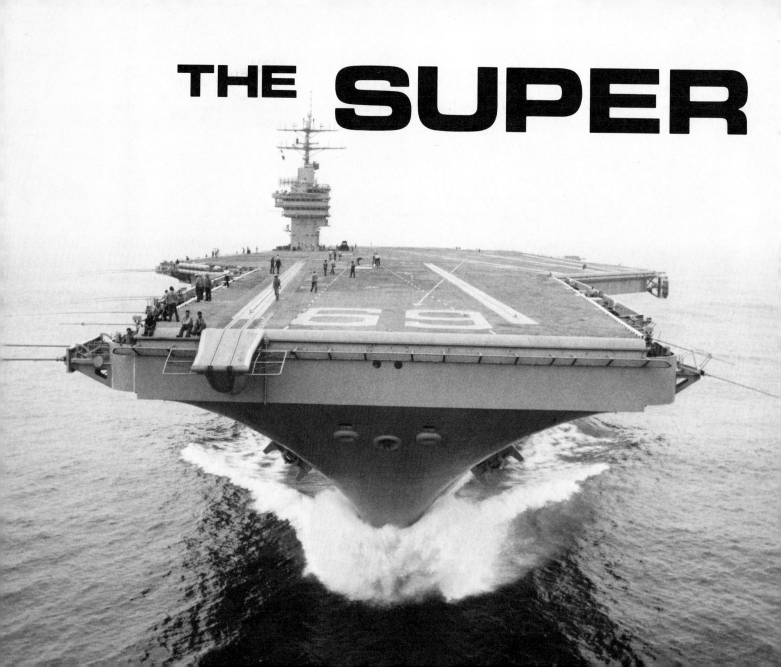

THE SUPER

CARRIERS

GEORGE SULLIVAN

Illustrated with photographs, diagrams, and maps

DODD, MEAD & COMPANY / NEW YORK

PICTURE CREDITS

Department of Defense, 96 (right); Library of Congress, 13; maps by Dyno Lowenstein, 42, 94; Newport News Shipbuilding and Dry Dock Company, 136, 147, 150, 151; George Sullivan, 92 (left), 93, 117, 119, 120, 121, 122, 123, 125, 126, 127, 129, 131, 143, 145; U.S. Air Force, 39, 40. All other photographs are Official U.S. Navy photographs.

1   2   3   4   5   6   7   8   9   10

Library of Congress Cataloging in Publication Data

Sullivan, George, 1927-
    The supercarriers.

    Includes index.
    SUMMARY: Presents the history of aircraft carriers, including their role during war, life on a carrier today, and the current controversy concerning carriers.
    1. Aircraft carriers—History—Juvenile literature. 2. United States. Navy—History—20th century—Juvenile literature. [1. Aircraft carriers—History. 2. United States. Navy—History—20th century] I. Title.
V874.3.S94   359.8'3   79-24304
ISBN 0-396-07794-3

Acknowledgments

The author is grateful to several individuals who were helpful to him in the preparation of this book, especially Captain Clark N. Gammel and Lieutenant James M. Kudla, U.S. Navy Office of Information, New York; Anna C. Urband, Department of the Navy, Washington, D.C.; Miles C. Wiley, Department of the Air Force, Kelly Air Force Base, Texas; and Thomas J. Olds, Newport News Shipbuilding, Newport News, Virginia.

Contents

A stern view of the *Nimitz* as vessel cruises waters of the Mediterranean.

1/

The Airplane Goes to Sea

Supercarriers are the biggest warships ever built. A carrier captain was once asked what it is like to operate such a vessel. "It is like steering Central Park," he said, "from the top of the Empire State Building."

The newest supercarriers are those of the *Nimitz* class—the *Nimitz* itself, the *Eisenhower,* and the *Vinson.* Each is home to over 6,000 Navy men and, as such, a small floating city.

The flight deck of the *Nimitz* is so big that three football games could be played end-to-end on it. Within the decks below, where there are miles and miles of intersecting corridors, it takes newcomers several days to be able to find their way around.

The *Nimitz,* named in honor of Fleet Admiral Chester W. Nimitz, a hero of World War II, is one of a handful of the Navy's nuclear-powered surface vessels. Its two reactors can drive the ship at more than 30 knots, remarkable speed for a ship of its size. Those reactors will enable the *Nimitz* to operate for more than 13 years without having to refuel. In that time, the ship will travel more than 800,000 miles.

The ship's 100 airplanes include swift jet fighters and attack aircraft, antisubmarine planes with sophisticated detection equipment, and top-secret reconnaissance aircraft.

When the *Nimitz* puts out to sea, it is loaded with enough provisions for 90 days, including 90,000 dozens of eggs, 243,000 pounds of meat, and ingredients for one million pancakes.

The ship has its own telephone system with over 2,000 numbers, a television studio to provide programs for the crew, a shopping "mall" with half a dozen stores, a laundry, barber shops, snack bars, hobby shops, a library, and gymnasium.

It has its own hospital with four doctors, two fully equipped operating rooms, and beds for 80 patients. Its dental department treats 200 patients a week.

To give the *Nimitz* its no-nonsense appearance, 672 gallons of gray paint and 104 gallons of black paint have been used to cover its exterior surfaces.

The *Nimitz* was one of twelve supercarriers in operation at the beginning of the 1980s. Two other smaller carriers were also on active duty, but scheduled for early retirement.

The twelve supercarriers are the centerpiece of America's 450-ship Navy. They are the principal means by which the Navy carries out its mandate of ensuring the free use of the sea lanes and, if necessary, projecting its power ashore.

Aircraft carriers have not always played such a vital role. It was not until World War II that the aircraft carrier replaced the battleship as the foremost instrument of naval warfare. The turning point was the Battle of the Coral Sea, where, for the first time, carrier planes were able to strike, and strike with stunning effect, over long distances.

Aircraft carriers were called upon again during the Korean War and the war in Vietnam.

Carriers of the 1980s are much different from those of the past. Their size is the chief difference. To be able to accommodate fast and powerful jet aircraft, carriers have had to grow much bigger.

Today, the role of these huge vessels is being questioned. Have they become *too* big? In the case of enemy missile attack, would they be mere "sitting ducks"? Is it practical to make them nuclear-powered? Are they worth their enormous cost? This book seeks to answer these questions.

The Wright brothers' first powered flight at Kitty Hawk in 1903 had scarcely been completed when some

Overhead view of the nuclear-powered U.S.S. *Eisenhower*, one of the Navy's newest *Nimitz*-class carriers.

military experts began to view the airplane as a war machine. Not only could it be made to serve as a land-based weapon, they reasoned, it could also be operated from a ship at sea.

The idea of a ship to carry aircraft might even be said to predate the Wright brothers. Clement Ader, a French aviator, in a book titled *L'Aviation Militaire,* published in 1895, described what such a ship might look like: "To start with, the deck will have to be cleared of any obstacles; it will be a flat area, as wide as possible, not conforming to the lines of the hull, and will resemble a landing strip.

"The speed of this ship will have to be at least as great as that of cruisers or even greater.

"Servicing of the aircraft will have to be done below deck. Access to this lower deck will be by means of a lift long enough and wide enough to take an aircraft with wings folded.

"Along the sides will be the workshops of the mechanics responsible for refitting the planes and for keeping them ready for flight."

It was to be another fifteen years before aircraft were developed that could demonstrate whether Ader's ideas had any practical value.

Of course, before a ship could be designed to carry airplanes, the value of airplanes themselves had to be proven. Officials of the U.S. Navy had doubts about them.

Navy observers had watched aircraft in flight in 1907 at the Jamestown (Virginia) Exposition, and again in 1908 when the Wright brothers were conducting test flights at Fort Myers, Florida. They were not impressed. Afterward, they declared that such experiments "had not achieved sufficient importance" to win the Navy's support.

This type of thinking began to change in 1910, thanks to Glenn H. Curtiss, an American inventor and aviator. Curtiss was the first man to fly a full mile at a public exhibition, a feat that he accomplished in 1908.

Two years later, Curtiss won national acclaim and a $10,000 prize that had been posted by the New York *World* by making a 142-mile flight from Albany to New York City. Afterward, the *World* declared: "The battles of the future will be fought in the air. The aeroplane will decide the future of nations."

The newspaper arranged for a bombing range to be set up on Lake Keuka, near Curtiss' home in Hammondsport, New York. Floats were anchored on the lake surface to form the outline of a battleship.

Curtiss flew over the target and dropped 15 simulated bombs onto it, as reporters from the *World* watched. "An airplane costing a few thousand dollars," said the newspaper, "is able to destroy a battleship costing many millions."

The Navy began waking up.

In September, 1910, Captain Irving W. Chambers was made officer-in-charge of naval aviation. Not long after his appointment, Chambers and Curtiss met at an aviation show at Halethorpe. Maryland, Chambers was also introduced to a twenty-four-year-old Curtiss test pilot named Eugene Ely, who made his living by flying planes in air shows. Before the year was out, Ely, Chambers, and Curtiss were to make aviation history.

At about the time of the Chambers-Curtiss meeting, a German steamship line announced it was making

In first carrier landing and first takeoff, test pilot Eugene Ely was at the controls.

preparations to launch an airplane from one of its vessels to test ship-to-shore mail delivery. This news upset Captain Chambers. Since the airplane was an American invention, Captain Chambers felt that any advance in its operation should be properly made by Americans, not by any foreign power.

Chambers immediately sought and was granted permission to attempt an aircraft launching from the U.S.S. *Birmingham,* a light cruiser. A wooden platform not much bigger than a tennis court—83 feet long, 24 feet wide—was constructed on the ship's foredeck to serve as a take-off strip.

Chambers asked the Wright brothers whether they would like to take part in the experiment. They declined.

It was then that Chambers remembered Curtiss and Ely. He found them eager to participate. Besides their enthusiasm, they even had a plane, the same spindly biplane—a Curtiss Model D—that Curtiss himself had piloted on his prize-winning flight from Albany to New York. It was known as the *Albany Flyer.*

Like the Wright brothers' plane, the *Flyer* was a fragile-looking craft, put together of wood, wire, and cotton fabric. Only 26 feet in length, it had a nose shaped like a box kite and a big rudder at the tail. The pilot's seat was in the open, fixed to the leading edge of the lower wing.

The flight was scheduled for November 14, 1910. A big crane hoisted the *Albany Flyer* onto the deck of the *Birmingham* at the Norfolk Naval Shipyard. When the plane was rolled into take-off position on the wooden runway, its front wheel was only 57 feet from the platform end.

Curtiss had modified the aircraft for its over-the-water flight by having a pair of floats installed beneath the wings. He also attached a long bag filled with corks to the plane's center keel.

The *Birmingham* steamed out of the harbor and headed a few miles north toward Chesapeake Bay. There the ship dropped anchor.

The day was raw and overcast. As Curtiss and Ely worked to ready the plane for its flight, they felt rain sprinkling down. There was even some hail.

The plan was the *Birmingham* to head into the wind at the time Ely attempted his takeoff. If there were 15 knots of headwind, and if the *Birmingham* was steaming at 15 knots, it would create the same amount of lift as if the plane were going 30 knots faster than its actual speed. This would make up for the abbreviated runway.

The rain got heavier and visibility got worse. Ely fretted, pacing back and forth on the open deck.

Around 2:30 in the afternoon, the sky brightened and the rain ceased. But weather stations were reporting that more rain and strong winds were on the way. It was now or probably never, Ely decided.

Orders were given to raise the ship's anchor. As the heavy deck windlass began noisily to haul up the anchor chain, Ely clambered into the pilot's seat. He adjusted the football helmet he wore for safety, and checked the inflated bicycle inner tube about his waist.

He tested the plane's controls. The anchor, at the end of more than 500 feet of heavy chain, was still being raised.

Ely instructed his mechanic to spin the prop and start the engine. He adjusted his goggles. He tested the controls once more. He could hear the windlass turning and the anchor chain clanking through the hawsepipe onto the deck.

Giant crane hoists Ely's plane to the deck of the *Birmingham*.

As he peered to the south and west, the direction in which he was to fly, Ely saw dark clouds gathering. His heart began to pound. Meanwhile, his chattering engine was using precious gasoline.

Finally, Ely could not stand it any longer. When he turned and looked back toward the bridge, there were no signs that anything was happening. It didn't seem that the anchor was about to be raised or the ship was going to be moving soon.

Ely signaled his mechanic to remove the plane's wooden wheel chocks. The man hesitated, knowing that no takeoff was to be attempted until the ship was underway. Ely signaled the man again, and scowled angrily.

This time the mechanic followed instructions. Ely gunned the engine. The *Albany Flyer* hurried down the deck. Rain peppered Ely's face and goggles, obscuring his vision.

At the end of the runway, the *Flyer* lifted into the air, but then suddenly dipped dangerously, rolling to one side. The floats and the plane's wheels skimmed the water's surface, jolting Ely and splashing salt water in his face. He struggled with the controls in an effort to keep the plane in the air.

Slowly the *Flyer* leveled off and began gaining altitude. Ely headed west for land.

Then another problem developed. The plane's wooden propeller had also struck the water, and one of its tips was shattered. The out-of-balance prop started the whole plane vibrating.

One close call had been enough for Ely. At the first sight of land, he set the crippled plane down. It happened to be a sandy strip of beach known as Willoughby Spit, about 2½ miles from Norfolk. There ended what is perhaps the most notable flight in the history of naval aviation.

For his landmark effort, Ely received $500 from John B. Ryan, a wealthy publisher, in return for the splintered propeller. He also received a letter of thanks from the Secretary of the Navy.

But Ely's achievement caused no policy changes. As far as the Navy was concerned, the airplane was still not to be taken seriously.

Captain Chambers, delighted with the success of the first "launching" from the *Birmingham,* now became interested in demonstrating it was practical to land a plane on a warship. Curtiss and Ely would again be involved. Curtiss would supply the plane, a Curtiss D-IV Military, a craft similar in appearance to the *Albany Flyer,* but with a larger amount of wing space. Ely would do the piloting.

A different ship and a different location were chosen for this experiment. The ship was a cruiser, the U.S.S. *Pennsylvania.* The location was San Francisco Bay.

The landing platform for the experiment was constructed at the Mare Island Naval Shipyard, not far from San Francisco. The platform, 120 feet long, 32 feet wide, was designed to fit on the afterdeck of the *Pennsylvania,* that section from the mainmast and stacks to the ship's stern. It would cover all deck equipment and the gun turrets.

As a safety measure, the platform was made to slope sharply upward at the end, where a big canvas screen was installed. In addition, canvas was lashed to the sides of the deck to serve as a safety netting should the plane veer out of control.

Ely's Curtiss biplane lumbers into the air from the U.S.S. *Birmingham.*

Hook dangling from Ely's plane grappled ropes connecting sandbags that lined sides of specially constructed deck, braking plane's speed.

As a final precaution, a simple and yet ingenious arrester system to slow the plane's deck speed was devised. Modern recovery operations involving fast and powerful jet aircraft bear a strong resemblance to this original system.

It consisted of 22 ropes that were strung across the width of the newly installed flight deck. The ropes were fixed to timbers which held them about four inches above the deck's surface. Each rope was tied to two 50-pound sandbags, one at each end.

The Curtiss plane was equipped with three sets of metal hooks, which dangled down from between the aircraft's landing wheels. What was supposed to happen, of course, was that the hooks were to snag the lines as the plane came in for its landing, and the weight of the sandbags would then brake its forward progress.

As with the *Albany Flyer,* Curtiss attached two floats to the underside of each of the plane's wings. Ely's safety equipment was upgraded. Instead of a bicycle inner tube around his waist, he wore a pair of inflated motorcycle inner tubes about his chest and under his arms.

On January 18, 1911, Ely took off from San Francisco's Presidio Field, and headed out over the Bay where the *Pennsylvania* steamed. A light crosswind was blowing as Ely approached the deck, but he skillfully steadied his craft, then went gliding in at a speed estimated to be around 40 miles an hour.

As he cleared the lip of the deck, Ely pulled up the nose of the plane slightly to lose some speed. The grappling hooks missed the first 11 lines, but caught the twelfth. Quickly the plane's speed diminished, and it pulled to a full stop 50 feet from the end of the deck and the canvas screen.

Less than an hour later, the aircraft was turned around so as to head in the opposite direction. The ropes and sandbags were removed from the deck. Ely raced the plane down the runway, into the air, and back to the Presidio.

Later in 1911, Ely was killed in an air crash. His efforts in establishing the airplane as a ship-based weapon gained some measure of recognition in 1926 when he was posthumously awarded the Distinguished Flying Cross.

In the years that followed Ely's achievements, little was done on behalf of naval aviation. The battleship, the most powerful ship of the day, was supreme. Battleship admirals had no wish to have the decks of their ships cluttered with airplanes and the equipment they required. No one had the inclination, nor was there money available, to build a ship just for airplanes.

During World War I, naval aviation went off in another direction. The United States entered the war in April, 1917. That month, Rear Admiral W. S. Sims, the officer in charge of naval forces in European waters,

appealed for airplanes, but the airplanes he asked for were seaplanes. A seaplane is one equipped with floats, which enables it to take off from land or on water.

German submarines were sinking great numbers of American and British merchant ships. Admiral Sims believed that seaplanes could be useful in antisubmarine warfare.

What Sims and the other naval officials really wanted was some kind of super seaplane, one that was big enough to carry sufficient fuel to enable it to make the transoceanic flight. What was the use of building a seaplane in the United States, then putting it aboard a cargo ship for delivery to England, if German submarines were likely to sink the ship? A large number of aircraft bound for England were already strewn about the ocean bottom.

The Royal Navy had successfully experimented with seaplanes. At first, small vessels would carry three or four seaplanes into the area where they were needed. A crane would then lower them one by one into the water, and they would take off and carry out their missions. These small ships were called seaplane tenders.

Their failing was that they could only launch and recover aircraft when the water was calm. When storms prevailed and the sea grew angry, seaplanes were useless.

To solve this problem, the British fitted out the liner *Campania* with a flight deck that was 230 feet in length. Auxiliary wheels were fastened to a seaplane to enable it to take off from the deck, wheels that the pilot released as soon as he was in the air.

The British also experimented with barges as seaplane carriers. The planes were loaded into barges which were then towed to within striking distance of targets that had been selected. Then a rear compartment in each barge was flooded, and the planes floated. They took off, bombed their targets, and returned to their land base.

Toward the end of World War I, the *Furious,* originally a light cruiser, refitted with a flat-surfaced deck, joined the British fleet. On August 2, 1917, a Sopworth Pup landed aboard. Since there was no mechanical means of stopping the plane before it reached the end of the deck, crewmen grasped lines hanging from the plane's wing tips; as soon as the pilot cut the motor, they tugged the plane to a halt.

Before the war ended, the British reached the conclusion that land planes had many advantages over awkward seaplanes, and turned their efforts toward developing vessels that could take light land planes to sea.

Out of these efforts came the carrier *Argus,* completed in September, 1918, as World War I was drawing to a close. The *Argus* was truly a "flat top," with no masts, no stacks, and no superstructure. Several years later, when the first United States aircraft carrier went into service, it would closely resemble the *Argus* in both design and appearance.

2/

The Langley and Beyond

On November 11, 1918, when the Armistice was signed ending World War I, Great Britain ranked as the world leader in carrier development. The United States lagged far behind.

But in 1919, the Secretary of the Navy went before Congressional committees to seek funds to convert a six-year-old coal-carrying ship into an aircraft carrier.

This was a period when oil was replacing coal as fuel for steam turbines, and coal-carrying ships—colliers, as they were called—weren't needed anymore. Congress granted the Navy the small amount of money needed to make the conversion.

The *Jupiter,* as the collier was named, was not the perfect vessel. The ship had a top speed of only 14 knots, which was considered turtlelike, even by standards of the 1920s.

But the vessel's enormous storage spaces, which had been used for hauling coal, could easily and inexpensively be refitted for use as aircraft hangars. They could also be used for gasoline and ammunition storage, for spare engines and spare parts, and all the other gear that air operations required.

In March, 1920, the *Jupiter* lumbered into the Norfolk Navy Yard. There the vessel's coal-handling equipment was ripped out and a wooden flight deck that was 542 feet in length, almost as long as two football fields, was laid down.

What was unusual about the deck, when compared with carriers that were to come, is that it was completely free of any obstructions. Standing on the deck was like standing on an open highway—a wooden highway, to be sure.

An elevator was installed to lift planes from the storage deck to the flight deck. Two cranes were placed on the hangar deck, one on either side of the ship, to be used in hoisting seaplanes aboard.

The work took two years. In March, 1922, when the vessel was ready to leave the Navy Yard and go to sea again, it was renamed the U.S.S. *Langley,* honoring Samuel P. Langley, a pioneer in the theory and construction of heavier-than-air machines.

Besides their names, Navy ships are also identified by letters and numbers. D, for example, has always been used for destroyers, C for cruisers, and SS for submarines. When the *Langley* went into service, the ship was designated a CV, and thus became CV-1.

The C stood for carrier. The V indicated aviation. Of course, the letter A would have been more appropriate to indicate the word aviation, but at the time the letters CA were being used to identify heavy

The Navy's first carrier, the U.S.S. *Langley*.

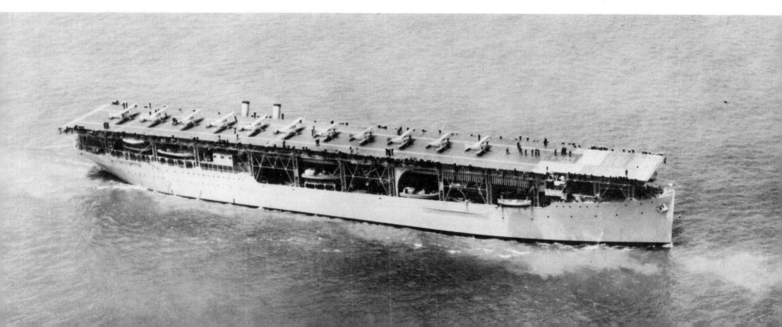

cruisers, the A standing for armored. All carriers since the *Langley* have carried the CV designation.

Sailors of the day seldom referred to the *Langley* by either its name or number, but called the ship the "Covered Wagon," because of its long, long "roof." In October, 1922, the first flights were made from the vessel and the first landings successfully completed.

For the next five years, the *Langley* was the only aircraft carrier the Navy owned. And for most of that period, it served an experimental role, testing aircraft and their related equipment.

The science of carrier operations was slow in developing. The arrester system that was used aboard the *Langley* in braking incoming aircraft was not much advanced from that employed by Eugene Ely in negotiating the very first carrier landing some eleven years before.

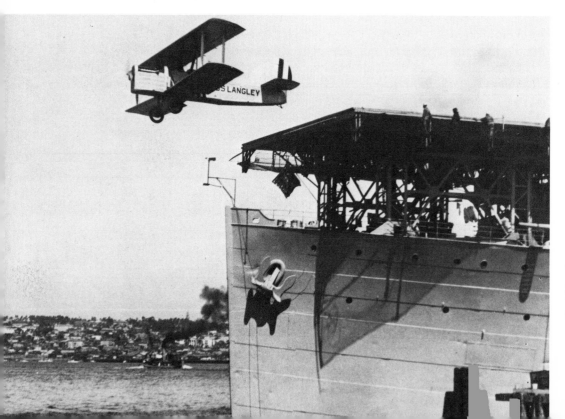

The *Langley* was invited to join fleet exercises in March, 1925. This photo was taken the following month.

The *Langley,* its flight deck crowded with aircraft, at Pearl Harbor in 1928.

The primitive nature of the landing system led to a condition known as "instrument face," a distinguishing feature of many of the *Langley*'s pilots. It was typified by flattened noses, scarred foreheads, and loosened teeth, caused when their faces smashed into the aircraft instrument panel during landings.

Planes hurtled over the side and into the water. They piled into the crash barriers. They toppled over onto their noses and came apart. Being a carrier pilot in those days was not a job for the nervous or fearful.

U.S.S. *Lexington* (CV-2) under construction.

The *Lexington* launches Martin T4M torpedo planes. Notice vessel's heavy weaponry.

But little by little, the landing system was improved and strengthened. Pilots themselves became more skilled.

By March, 1925, the *Langley* was so highly thought of that the vessel was invited to join fleet exercises for the first time. Scouting flights from the carrier became standard procedure. So impressed were naval officials that they recommended the construction of two additional aircraft carriers.

These two vessels were constructed upon two battle cruiser keels that had already been laid. Named the U.S.S. *Lexington* (CV-2) and U.S.S. *Saratoga* (CV-3), they joined the fleet in 1927. Most of the carriers built over the next few decades would follow the lead of the *Lexington* and *Saratoga,* in that they were named after notable battles. When there was an exception, it was usually to honor a fighting ship.

At the time, the *Lexington* and *Saratoga,* each at 33,000 tons, rated as the biggest, most powerful carriers

U.S.S. *Saratoga* (CV-3) in San Francisco Bay, 1930.

in the world. With an overall length of 901 feet, each was half again as long as the *Langley,* and they each carried twice as many planes as the old "Covered Wagon." The new carriers were capable of steaming along at 33¼ knots. The *Langley* could hardly generate half that speed.

Despite these advances, the Navy's admirals still did not look upon carrier aircraft as being very reliable, either in defending themselves or the ship. They made these new vessels carry much the same armament as battle cruisers carried. Eight 8-inch guns were installed in four turrets. Two of the turrets were mounted forward of the carrier's superstructure, and the two others aft of the stack.

The stack, a huge structure, as tall as a nine-story building, was actually an enclosure for four different stacks. In addition to its big guns, each of the new carriers was fitted out with a dozen 5-inch antiaircraft guns.

The idea that aircraft carriers had to be as heavily armed as battle cruisers was finally abandoned in 1934 when the U.S.S. *Ranger* (CV-4) was commissioned. The *Ranger* had no big guns, nor has any carrier since. The Navy policy makers had arrived at the belief that an aircraft carrier was meant to serve its aircraft, period. Battleships, cruisers, and destroyers could be provided to protect the carrier from surface attack.

Hangar deck of the U.S.S. *Saratoga*.

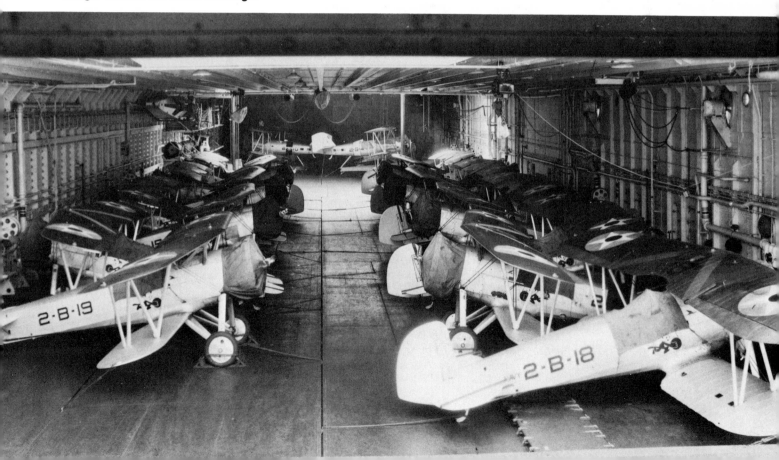

Carriers would continue to be equipped with antiaircraft guns, however, since the escort vessels were often not close enough to provide protective cover against aerial attack.

The *Ranger,* at 14,500 tons, was a much smaller vessel than either the *Lexington* or *Saratoga,* but its flight deck was almost as long—769 feet as compared to 888 feet—and it carried an equal number of planes.

The original plans called for the *Ranger* to have a completely flush deck, with no stack enclosure, and no island. But as the plans finally developed, a small island was included in the design. The stacks, however, were placed below flight deck level at the ship's stern.

As world tensions built during the 1930s and early 1940s, the United States built four more carriers. These included the *Yorktown* (CV-5), *Enterprise* (CV-6), and *Hornet* (CV-8), each with a displacement of

19,800 tons. The fourth carrier, the *Wasp* (CV-7), was smaller, at 14,700 tons.

The *Wasp*, the last of the new carriers to be commissioned, joined the fleet in 1941. That gave the Navy seven operational carriers, the *Langley* having been assigned duties as a seaplane tender. Before the year was out, all carriers, new and old, were going to be desperately needed.

On December 7, 1941, a sunny Sunday, much of the U.S. Pacific Fleet, a total of 86 vessels anchored at Pearl Harbor, Hawaii, was suddenly attacked by 100 Japanese airplanes and a number of submarines.

The battleship *Arizona* was sunk. Four other battleships, three destroyers, and one minelayer were severely damaged. Also damaged, but ultimately repaired and returned to service, were three battleships and three cruisers. Approximately 200 American airplanes were lost.

CARRIERS COMPLETED BEFORE WORLD WAR II

NAME	NUMBER	YEAR COMPLETED	*DISPLACEMENT (Tons)	LENGTH OF FLIGHT DECK (Feet)
Langley	CV-1	1922	11,000	542
Lexington	CV-2	1927	33,000	888
Saratoga	CV-3	1927	33,000	888
Ranger	CV-4	1934	14,500	769
Yorktown	CV-5	1937	19,800	810
Enterprise	CV-6	1938	19,800	810
Wasp	CV-7	1940	14,700	741
Hornet	CV-8	1941	19,800	810

*The size of Navy ships is stated in terms of displacement tons. Imagine lowering a ship in a closed dock brimming with water. Some of the water would spill over the dock's sides, that is, be displaced by the hull.

It is a law of physics that the ship would be buoyed up by a force equal in weight to the amount of water displaced, which is expressed in tons. A displacement ton is equal to 2,240 pounds.

 The Army and Navy suffered more than 4,500 casualties, including 2,343 men killed.

 Within twenty-four hours, the United States was an active participant in World War II. In the great rush of events that took place during the early months of the war, the *Langley* became a tragic participant.

 Classified as an auxiliary ship, the *Langley* was in the Pacific, in the Philippines, at the time the United States was thrust into the war. When the Japanese unleashed their assault upon the Philippines, the *Langley* headed south toward the safety of Australian waters.

Late in February, 1942, the *Langley* was assigned to transport P-40 fighter planes from Australia north and west to Java. The ship came under attack by nine Japanese land-based bombers. One bomb after another found its target. Fires broke out. Water flooded into the ship's holds and engine room spaces. Steering control was lost and the ship developed a scary list.

Commander R. P. McConnel, captain of the *Langley,* ordered the ship to be abandoned. A pair of destroyers rescued the *Langley*'s crew members and the pilots who were being carried as passengers.

The *Langley* might have sunk of its own accord, but the Americans didn't want to take a chance of the ship falling into Japanese hands, so torpedoes were fired into its hull. Moments later, the *Langley* slipped beneath the surface, a sad ending for a proud vessel.

U.S.S. *Wasp* (CV-7) joined the fleet in 1941, giving the Navy seven operational carriers.

Before World War II, battleships such as the U.S.S. *Iowa*, pictured here, were the Navy's mightiest weapons.

3/

The Carrier Goes to War

For most of the first half of the twentieth century, the battleship reigned as queen of the seas. No ship was more heavily gunned, none more heavily armored.

At the beginning of World War II, battleships carried as many as 10 huge guns, each with bores 16 inches in diameter and mounted in revolving turrets. Battleships such as the *Iowa* or *New Jersey* could fire those 16-inch projectiles any distance up to 23 miles. There were also secondary guns aboard, smaller in size, as well as heavy antiaircraft armament.

The battleship's armor protection was up to 19 inches thick in the main turrets and amidships, just below and above the waterline. The ship's superstructure was also heavily protected.

Battleships had enormous power, usually steam turbine or turbo-electric plants. The *Iowa* and other battleships of that class could steam along at a smart 35 knots.

No one hears about battleships today. The last active United States battleship, the *Wisconsin,* was decommissioned in 1958. At the time, only two other nations had warships of the battleship class. These vessels have since been scrapped or have found use as training ships.

The battleship was supreme so long as warfare was conducted on the surface of the sea. It could pound

the enemy with more firepower than any other vessel. It could absorb more punishment. But events that occurred in the Pacific Ocean in the first year of World War II were to put an end to the battleship era.

The devastation wrought by Japanese planes at Pearl Harbor had a ripple effect, dooming American forces in the Philippines and elsewhere.

In the months that followed the bombing, the Japanese moved swiftly. Before December was over, Japanese forces had overrun American garrisons on Wake Island and on Guam. Singapore and Java fell.

The Japanese also invaded the Philippines, quickly capturing Manila. They completed their Philippine conquest during April and May, 1942, when the last American forces on the Bataan peninsula and Corregidor surrendered.

Newspapers blared one Japanese success after another. Americans became discouraged.

By mid-1942, Japanese forces controlled the Pacific Ocean from their home islands as far east as Wake Island in the North Pacific. They were in command in the Marshall and Gilbert islands, south of Wake. They invaded New Guinea. They were bold enough to also strike far to the north, attacking the Aleutian Islands, now part of the state of Alaska. By June of 1942 they were in control of two of the Aleutians, Attu and Kiska.

Americans hungered for some good news. When it finally came, aircraft carriers helped to provide it.

There were three carriers assigned to Pacific waters in December, 1941. By a stroke of luck, none happened to be at Pearl Harbor when the Japanese planes struck. The *Lexington* was some 700 miles north and west of Pearl Harbor, transporting a squadron of Marine Corps pilots to Midway Island. The *Enterprise* had been on a similar mission, delivering Marine Corps planes to Wake Island, and was returning to Pearl Harbor at the time of the raid. The *Saratoga* was steaming in waters off San Diego.

The smoke had hardly cleared at Pearl Harbor when American military experts began planning a daring counterstrike. The newly commissioned carrier *Hornet* was to serve as the launching point for the attack.

The operation was cloaked in the utmost secrecy. Two dozen Air Force pilots were trained in making short takeoffs in their B-25 bombers, making them, in fact, in less space and less time than they had

At Pearl Harbor, flames and black smoke engulf battleships (left to right) *West Virginia, Tennessee,* **and** *Arizona.*

B-25s on board the *Hornet* while en route to their launching point for Tokyo attack.

believed possible. The airmen were never told why they were being so trained.

At a naval air station in San Francisco Bay in March, 1942, sixteen of these specially trained pilots watched as big cranes loaded their bombers one-by-one onto the flight deck of the *Hornet*. Since the planes were too big to fit into the hangar spaces, they had to be parked on the open deck. The ship headed out through the Golden Gate and into the open sea.

Two days later, the pilots were told what their mission was to be. Lieutenant Colonel James B. Doolittle, the officer in charge, gathered the pilots together in an empty mess hall of the *Hornet* and said to them:

"For the benefit of those of you who don't already know, or who have been guessing, we are going straight to Japan. The Navy is going to take us close as advisable, and we're going to take off from the deck. We're going to bomb Tokyo, Yokohama, Osaka, Kobe, and Nagoya."

The attack was planned for the night of April 18, but that morning the *Hornet* and its escort vessels were spotted by a Japanese patrol craft. Although the enemy ship was quickly sunk by Navy gunfire, it was feared the vessel might have radioed a warning to the Japanese. The bombers were ordered into the air immediately, even though the distance to Tokyo was 650 nautical miles, not 500 miles as had been originally planned.

Taking off from the carrier deck required courage and deft skills. The wingspan of a B-25 was 67 feet, which made the plane almost as wide as the carrier's flight deck. The biggest Navy fighter had a wingspan of 40 feet.

Normally, the bombers needed as much as 1,500 feet of runway to get into the air. The *Hornet* offered considerably less than half that distance.

A B-25 bomber soars from the *Hornet's* flight deck.

But the carrier's speed as the ship steamed into the wind was expected to make up for the runway's shortness. White lines were painted on the deck to guide the bomber pilots.

Still, taking off was a very ticklish business. One of the pilots, Captain Ted Lawson, in a book he wrote telling of the raid, titled *Thirty Seconds Over Tokyo,* described his takeoff in these terms:

The *Hornet* bit into the rough-house waves, dipping and rising until the flight deck was a crazy seesaw. Some of the waves were actually breaking over the deck. I had a brief fear of being hit by a wave on the takeoff and of crashing at the end of the deck and falling off into the path of the careening carrier.

Our wheel blocks were jerked out, and when I released the brakes we quivered forward, the wind grabbing at the wings. We rambled dangerously close to the edge, but I braked in time, got the left wheel back onto the white line and picked up speed.

Lieutenant Colonel Jimmy Doolittle, who led Tokyo raid, sits by the wing of his plane following crash landing in China.

Lawson first realized that he was airborne when he glanced down at where the white line on the deck should have been and saw water there. He banked, gaining altitude, and then, with his colleagues, set out for Tokyo.

Thirteen of the B-25s dropped 500-pound bombs on Tokyo and military bases in the area. The remaining three aircraft targeted on other Japanese industrial centers.

Because the planes were so big, they could not land on the deck of the *Hornet*. The pilots were assigned to proceed across Japan and the Sea of Japan and land in China, part of which was occupied by Japanese forces at the time.

The planes were never able to reach their assigned landing fields, and crashed or made forced landings. Nine of the 80 airmen who took part in the raid died, and two air crews fell into the hands of the Japanese. Several other airmen were seriously injured, including Captain Lawson, who crash-landed in China.

The surprise raid was a rude jolt to the Japanese. It embarrassed the Japanese leaders, who had promised the people their home islands would never be attacked. It also caused the Japanese to assign large defense forces to the protection of the islands. At the same time, it served to boost the morale of Americans.

While it achieved its goals, the raid was a one-of-a-kind occurrence. Military experts realized it would be foolhardy to attempt to use a carrier and big bombers in that manner again. A sea battle that took place just a few weeks later had a much more lasting influence on carrier history and development.

It was the Battle of the Coral Sea. The Coral Sea, a part of the South Pacific Ocean, lies just east of northeastern Australia and south of the Solomon Islands.

At the very time Jimmy Doolittle's bombers were on their way to Tokyo, the Japanese were mustering an enormous strike force to attack the Solomon Islands and southeastern New Guinea. If they could occupy the Solomons and Port Moresby in New Guinea, the Japanese realized they would open the door to an attack on the northeast coast of Australia.

To accomplish their goal, the Japanese assembled five separate invasion forces of transport ships and auxiliary vessels, and assigned each to attack at a different point within the area. To protect and support

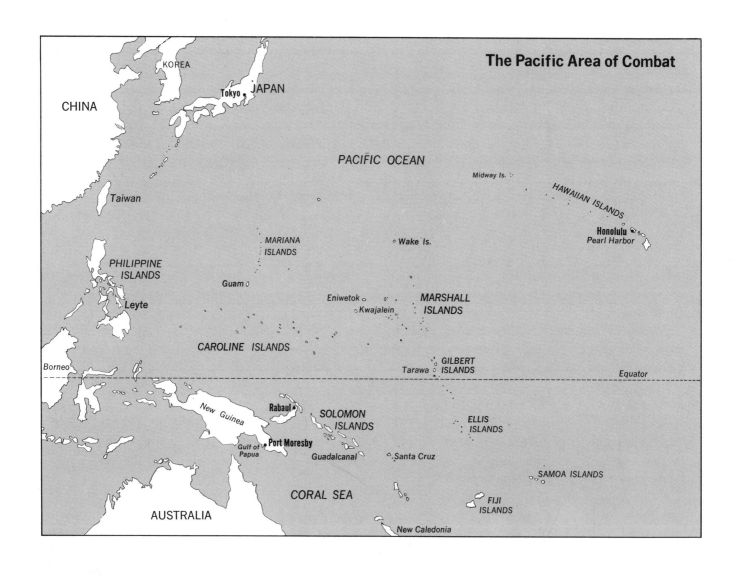

The Pacific Area of Combat

these invasion forces, the Japanese ordered two large carriers, one small carrier, 15 destroyers, and several gunboats into the Coral Sea.

The big carriers were the *Shokaku* and the *Zuikaku*. They carried a combined total of 126 aircraft. The smaller carrier, the *Shoho,* had 21 planes.

Fortunately, the Americans knew what was going on. From the first days of the war, United States intelligence experts had broken the Japanese naval code, and Admiral Chester Nimitz, commander of the Pacific forces, was able to be informed that a Japanese invasion force was soon to enter the Coral Sea. Nimitz presumed Port Moresby to be their target.

To oppose the Japanese naval force, Nimitz had only two carriers available, the *Lexington* and the *Yorktown.* The carrier *Saratoga* was undergoing repairs. The *Hornet* and *Enterprise* were returning from the western Pacific after the B-25 raid on Tokyo. But Nimitz was also able to summon 12 destroyers, six heavy cruisers, and two oilers into the area.

Rear Admiral Frank Jack Fletcher, posted aboard the *Yorktown,* took command of the American force. On May 7, Fletcher ordered search planes from the two carriers into the air. Shortly after, a scout plane reported sighting the smaller Japanese carrier, a light cruiser, and three gunboats.

Almost immediately, squadrons of SBD Dauntless bombers, F4F Wildcat fighters, and TBD Devastator

The Japanese carrier *Shoho* burns after torpedo plane attack during the Battle of the Coral Sea.

bombers took to the air from the two carriers. When the first American aircraft reached the target area, Japanese Zero fighters streaked up to intercept them. Below, the ships began maneuvering crazily to evade the American bombs and torpedoes.

But the evasive tactics did not help the carrier *Shoho*. Thirteen bombs and seven torpedoes ripped into the vessel's hull, and the *Shoho* was at the bottom within a matter of minutes. As the ship was sinking, Lieutenant Commander Robert Dixon, a pilot from the *Lexington*, radioed back to his ship: SCRATCH ONE FLATTOP!

All but three of the American aircraft returned to their carriers for rearming and refueling. Admiral Fletcher decided not to send them out against the cruiser and gunboats because the main Japanese force, bulwarked by the *Shokaku* and *Zuikaku*, had not been found.

Nor, of course, had the Japanese been able to discover where the American force was lurking. Then, early on the morning of May 8, a Japanese reconnaissance plane reported sighting the American carriers

Steam wells up from the littered deck of the *Lexington* at Battle of the Coral Sea.

Lexington burns after being hit by bombs and torpedoes.

and their escort vessels. The news was flashed to the Japanese aircraft and moments later they were in the air.

In perfect flying weather, 69 Japanese planes attacked the American force, concentrating their firepower on the two carriers, both of which began maneuvering wildly. But in their maneuvering, the two carriers became separated, dividing their escort vessels into two different groups. This was a fatal mistake. Instead of the carriers being able to screen each other from the Japanese onslaught, they were now vulnerable to attack from all sides.

Torpedo planes roared in on the *Lexington*. One torpedo ripped into the ship's hull on the port side forward. A minute later, a second torpedo exploded into the starboard side, also forward. Dozens of bombs

This, the last known photo of the *Lexington,* was taken after the fires aboard the vessel had been brought under control, but before the start of a series of explosions that ripped engine spaces apart, sending the ship to the bottom.

rained down on or near the vessel. Five scored direct hits. Near misses ruptured hull plates.

The attack lasted nine minutes. By the time it ended, fires were raging below decks and three of the ship's 16 boiler rooms were flooded. But within an hour, the fires had been extinguished and, quite miraculously, the *Lexington* was resuming flight operations.

Then suddenly and without warning massive explosions ripped the ship from stem to stern. The carrier's huge storage tanks that carried aviation fuel had been weakened during the attack, and explosive vapors had escaped to be ignited by a generator. One explosion followed another. New fires broke out inside the ship. Water mains were severed by the explosions, crippling fire-fighting efforts. Temperatures in the engine room spaces reached 160°F. There was no choice but to abandon the ship. Destroyers pulled alongside to rescue the survivors.

After everyone had left the ship, Admiral Fletcher ordered a destroyer to sink the burning hulk. Five torpedoes were fired and four exploded against the ship's sides. An hour later, the *Lexington* slid beneath the surface.

The *Yorktown* did not escape unharmed. An 800-pound bomb struck the ship's flight deck near the island, exploding deep within the vessel. The fires that it caused were quickly brought under control. But the blast caused extensive damage and killed 37 men.

While aircraft from the *Shokaku* and *Zuikaku* were battering the *Lexington* and *Yorktown,* the Japanese carriers came under the attack of American planes.

As the Americans approached, the *Zuikaku* entered a rain squall, and remained hidden from view. That left the *Shokaku* as the chief target, and American dive bombers and torpedo planes pounced upon the vessel.

But the torpedoes all missed the ship. Two bombs scored hits, one damaging the flight deck, the other wrecking an engine repair shop.

That afternoon, both forces began withdrawing from the area.

Who won the Battle of the Coral Sea? It was a scoreboard victory for the Japanese. The *Lexington* was sunk, the *Yorktown* damaged. An American destroyer and oiler were also sent to the bottom. An estimated

Heavily attacked at the Battle of the Coral Sea, the *Yorktown* escapes with damage that was quickly repaired.

Fire and damage on the *Yorktown* (CV-5) during the Battle of Midway. Ship eventually sank, but Japanese losses included four big carriers.

70 American combat planes were lost. By comparison, the Japanese lost one light carrier, a few support vessels, and 43 aircraft. The *Shokaku* returned to Japan for repairs.

From a tactical standpoint, it was an American victory, however. The Japanese assault against Port Moresby and northeastern New Guinea had been turned back. Australians could breathe a sigh of relief.

But no matter which nation is considered the victor, the Battle of the Coral Sea made history. It marked the first time warships participating in a naval engagement had neither seen or fired upon one another. Only pilots saw enemy ships.

No longer would the role of a carrier be that of a support vessel for battleships and cruisers. The engagement at the Coral Sea demonstrated that the carrier could be the Navy's long arm, striking again and again over long distances, whether the target happened to be on land or sea.

When land armies moved forward, they captured enemy airstrips or constructed airstrips of their own, so as to bring air power forward. It was a matter of efficiency. It reduced the time needed for refueling, rearming, and repairing aircraft. It shortened the trip to and from enemy targets.

The carrier now enabled the Navy to do the same thing. When a naval force moved forward, the airstrip now moved with it. Of course, the carrier provided more than just a mere airstrip. It also brought along the aircraft, the fuel, and the crew members to fly and service the planes.

An age-old prescription for military success advised "to get there firstest with the mostest." Carriers enabled military leaders to do just that.

The Battle of Midway, which took place in June, 1942, a month after the Coral Sea engagement, confirmed the dominant role that the carrier had attained. At Midway, planes from the *Yorktown*—hur-

Surrounded by F6F Hellcats, ordnancemen work on bombs on the hangar deck of the U.S.S. *Yorktown* (CV-10), while ship's officers watch motion picture.

U.S.S. *Essex* leads parade of warships through the waters of the South Pacific.

riedly repaired after the Battle of the Coral Sea—the *Enterprise,* and *Hornet* sank four big Japanese carriers, the *Akagi, Kaga, Hiryu,* and *Soryu.* Japanese losses also included a cruiser. The United States lost the *Yorktown* and a destroyer.

So great were their losses in ships and airplanes, the Japanese were put on the defensive for the first time. The Battle of Midway is recognized as the turning point in the war in the Pacific.

Even before the Japanese attack on Pearl Harbor, the Navy had begun a major carrier construction program. Once the war started, the program was speeded up, and carriers started coming out of the nation's shipyards on almost an assembly-line basis.

The Navy had learned much about carrier aviation since the days of the *Langley* and out of the experience gained in operating the *Lexington* and *Saratoga.* This knowledge went into the planning and design of the U.S.S. *Essex* (CV-9), the first in a new class of carriers.

The *Essex* was commissioned on the last day of 1942, a critical time in the Pacific theatre of war. Only two combat carriers were then in service, the *Saratoga,* which had been damaged and repaired, and the *Enterprise.*

The *Lexington* had gone down at the Battle of the Coral Sea. The *Yorktown* had been lost at Midway. The *Wasp* had been sunk in September, 1942, the *Hornet* a month later.

The *Essex* arrived in Hawaii in May, 1943, the first of much-needed carrier reinforcements. The *Essex* was about the size of the *Lexington* and *Saratoga,* and just as fast. Innovations included a longer and wider flight deck, more hangar space, and accommodations for as many as 100 aircraft, compared to the *Saratoga*'s 75 and the *Enterprise*'s 85.

The *Essex* bristled with antiaircraft firepower fore and aft, including 20 5-inch guns, 16 of them in twin mounts near the triangular-shaped island, and others mounted on catwalks that fringed the flight deck.

At about the same time the *Essex* joined the fleet, the second carrier of the class, the *Yorktown* (CV-10), named to honor the gallant ship sunk at Midway, was being launched. Other *Essex*-class carriers launched during 1943 included the *Intrepid* (CV-11), *Hornet* (CV-12), *Franklin* (CV-13), and *Wasp* (CV-18). In total, the Navy was to build 24 carriers of the *Essex* class.

WORLD WAR II ESSEX-CLASS CARRIERS

NAME	NUMBER	YEAR COMPLETED	DISPLACEMENT (Tons)	LENGTH OF FLIGHT DECK (Feet)
Essex	CV-9	1942	36,000	872
Yorktown	CV-10	1943	36,000	872
Intrepid	CV-11	1943	36,000	872
Hornet	CV-12	1943	36,000	872
Franklin	CV-13	1943	36,000	888
Ticonderoga	CV-14	1944	36,000	888
Randolph	CV-15	1944	36,000	888
Lexington	CV-16	1943	36,000	872
Bunker Hill	CV-17	1943	36,000	872
Wasp	CV-18	1943	36 000	872
Hancock	CV-19	1944	36,000	888
Bennington	CV-20	1944	36,000	872
Boxer	CV-21	1945	36,000	888
Bon Homme Richard	CV-31	1945	36,000	888
Leyte	CV-32	1946	36,000	888
Kearsarge	CV-33	1946	36,000	888
Oriskany	CV-34	1950	36,000	888
Reprisal	CV-35	(Cancelled)	—	—
Antietam	CV-36	1945	36,000	888
Princeton	CV-37	1945	36,000	888
Shangri-La	CV-38	1944	36,000	888
Lake Champlain	CV-39	1945	36,000	888
Tarawa	CV-40	1945	36,000	888

Name	Number	Year Completed	Displacement (Tons)	Length of Flight Deck (Feet)
Valley Forge	CV-45	1946	36,000	888
Iwo Jima	CV-46	(Cancelled)	—	—
Philippine Sea	CV-47	1946	36,000	888
(Unnamed)	CV-50 to CV-55	(Cancelled)	—	—

With these ships, a new carrier strategy developed. At the Battle of the Coral Sea and at Midway—throughout 1942, in fact—carriers operated singly or in pairs. But in 1943, naval strategists began to group them in three's and four's. Two or more such groups comprised a carrier task force.

A bombing plane approaches deck of U.S.S. *Ranger.*

Left: F6F Hellcats warm up for takeoff on deck of U.S.S. *Yorktown* (CV-10).

Right: Its guns manned and ready, U.S.S. *Lexington* (CV-16) accepts an F6F Hellcat during Battle of Saipan.

The new combat carriers went into action for the first time early in September, 1943, their planes bombing Marcus Island, then held by the Japanese. In the months that followed, a steady series of shattering raids and amphibious landings helped to wrest the Pacific from Japanese control. In almost every case, fighters, bombers, and torpedo planes spearheaded American gains. By 1945, the enemy had been forced back to the Asian mainland in a purely defensive position. When the atomic bomb attacks on

F6F Hellcats are launched from the deck of the U.S.S. *Randolph* **(CV-15) for an air strike against Japan.**

Hiroshima and Nagasaki ended the war, the Navy was preparing for the invasion of Japan and a drive upon Tokyo itself.

The *Essex* represented only one of several types of carriers built during World War II. Another type was the escort carrier, or CVE. These vessels were also called "jeep" carriers.

The first escort carrier, the U.S.S. *Long Island* (CVE-1), was built upon a hull originally planned for a merchant freighter. Construction of the *Long Island* took less than three months.

Once completed, the *Long Island* was used primarily as a training ship, as the *Langley* had been used years before. What the Navy learned in this period was put to use in the construction of 20 more CVEs that were ordered late in 1941.

Some CVEs were built on freighter hulls, as the *Long Island* had been. Others were constructed on tanker hulls. They were slow-moving vessels and could boast little in the way of protective armor. In total, 123 CVEs were built, 85 for the U.S. Navy, 38 for Great Britain.

The U.S.S. *Long Island* (CVE-1), first of the escort carriers.

ESCORT CARRIERS COMPLETED DURING WORLD WAR II

NAME	NUMBER	NAME	NUMBER
Long Island	CVE-1	Tripoli	CVE-64
Bogue	CVE-9	Wake Island	CVE-65
Card	CVE-11	White Plains	CVE-66
Copahee	CVE-12	Solomons	CVE-67
Core	CVE-13	Kalinin Bay	CVE-68
Nassau	CVE-16	Kasaan Bay	CVE-69
Altamaha	CVE-18	Fanshaw Bay	CVE-70
Barnes	CVE-20	Kitkun Bay	CVE-71
Block Island	CVE-21	Tulagi	CVE-72
Breton	CVE-23	Gambier Bay	CVE-73
Croatan	CVE-25	Nehenta Bay	CVE-74
Sangamon	CVE-26	Hoggatt Bay	CVE-75
Suwannee	CVE-27	Kadashan Bay	CVE-76
Chenango	CVE-28	Marcus Island	CVE-77
Santee	CVE-29	Savo Island	CVE-78
Prince William	CVE-31	Ommaney Bay	CVE-79
Casablanca	CVE-55	Petrof Bay	CVE-80
Liscome Bay	CVE-56	Rudyerd Bay	CVE-81
Anzio	CVE-57	Saginaw Bay	CVE-82
Corregidor	CVE-58	Sargent Bay	CVE-83
Mission Bay	CVE-59	Shamrock Bay	CVE-84
Guadalcanal	CVE-60	Shipley Bay	CVE-85
Manila Bay	CVE-61	Sitkoh Bay	CVE-86
Natoma Bay	CVE-62	Steamer Bay	CVE-87
St. Lo	CVE-63	Cape Esperance	CVE-88

NAME	NUMBER		NAME	NUMBER
Takansis Bay	CVE-89		Gilbert Islands	CVE-107
Thetis Bay	CVE-90		Kula Gulf	CVE-108
Makassar Strait	CVE-91		Cape Gloucester	CVE-109
Windham Bay	CVE-92		Salerno Bay	CVE-110
Makin Island	CVE-93		Vella Gulf	CVE-111
Lunga Point	CVE-94		Siboney	CVE-112
Bismarck Sea	CVE-95		Puget Sound	CVE-113
Salamaua	CVE-96		Rendova	CVE-114
Hollandia	CVE-97		Bairoko	CVE-115
Kwajalein	CVE-98		Badoeng Strait	CVE-116
Admiralty Islands	CVE-99		Saidor	CVE-117
Bougainville	CVE-100		Sicily	CVE-118
Matanikau	CVE-101		Point Cruz	CVE-119
Attu	CVE-102		Mindoro	CVE-120
Rai	CVE-103		Rabaul	CVE-121
Munda	CVE-104		Palau	CVE-122
Commencement Bay	CVE-105		Tinian	CVE-123
Block Island	CVE-106			

Their big job was protecting huge convoys of merchant vessels bound from the United States for Europe from submarine attack. In the early months of World War II, German undersea raiders hovered near the American coastal ports, picking off ships, sometimes while they were still in sight of land. Before long, however, land-based aircraft drove the submarines far out to sea. But once in mid-ocean, beyond the range of land-based aircraft, the ships once again fell victim to the undersea marauders.

Escort carriers, accompanying the convoys, helped to save the day. Planes from the carriers would scout ahead of the clustered merchant ships and tankers, searching out the submarines before they could attack.

Some wartime carriers were built on cruiser keels. U.S.S. *Langley* (CVL-27), in foreground, was one such vessel.

Eventually, the escort carriers overcame the German submarine threat in the North Atlantic.

Escort carriers were also used in transporting huge numbers of assembled aircraft to various parts of the world where the war raged.

They also supported amphibious landings in the capture of the Gilbert Islands and Marshall Islands. They later supported landings in the retaking of the Philippine Islands. Escort carrier aircraft conducted hundreds upon hundreds of air strikes during the Okinawa campaign, the last and most violent amphibious engagement of the war.

By the end of the war, these vessels had outgrown the designation of "escort" carrier. The Navy ordered that they be reclassified as full-fledged combat ships.

Still another type of carrier built during World War II was the light carrier, or CVL. Built on a cruiser hull, the light carrier was bigger and faster than an escort carrier, but smaller than an *Essex*-class vessel. Nine CVLs were built during World War II.

LIGHT CARRIERS COMPLETED DURING WORLD WAR II

NAME	NUMBER	COMPLETED	DISPLACEMENT (Tons)	LENGTH OF FLIGHT DECK (Feet)
Independence	CVL-22	1943	15,100	622
Princeton	CVL-23	1943	15,100	622
Belleau Wood	CVL-24	1943	15,100	622
Cowpens	CVL-25	1943	15,100	622
Monterey	CVL-26	1943	15,100	622
Langley	CVL-27	1943	15,100	622
Cabot	CVL-28	1943	15,100	622
Bataan	CVL-29	1943	15,100	622
San Jacinto	CVL-30	1943	15,100	622

At the end of World War II, the United States possessed the mightiest Navy any nation had ever assembled. It consisted of some 1,500 combatant ships, a figure that included 111 carriers of all types. In the minds of everyone, the carrier was now recognized as the backbone of the fleet. It was carrier aviation's finest hour.

4/

Bigger and Better

In the years that immediately followed World War II, few people ever questioned the dominant role in which aircraft carriers had been cast. If anything, that role was broadened, and carriers constructed in the postwar period were much bigger than *Essex*-class ships. They had to be bigger to be able to accommodate modern jet aircraft.

The first of the postwar carriers was the *Midway* (CV-41), the lead ship in a class that included the *Franklin D. Roosevelt* (CV-42) and the *Coral Sea* (CV-43).

The *Roosevelt* gained special recognition on July 21, 1946, when an FD-1 Phantom put down on its flight deck. It marked the first successful carrier landing for a jet airplane.

Construction of *Midway*-class ships had actually begun during World War II, and reflected some of the lessons learned during the war. Early carrier losses were caused by the failure to control fire and flooding sustained during an attack. So carriers of the *Midway* class were built sturdier. They were also fast ships, able to cruise at 33 knots. They could carry as many as 137 planes, more planes than any other previous carrier.

Each ship of the *Midway* class had a flight deck 977 feet long and 136 feet wide, 105 feet longer and 20

The introduction of jet aircraft triggered the need for much bigger carriers. Here an XFD-1 Phantom completes the first carrier jet-qualification test aboard the *Franklin D. Roosevelt.*

feet wider than *Essex*-class carriers. *Midway*-class ships were originally known as battle carriers, but later that designation was dropped.

But even as the *Midway*-class carriers were becoming operational, some military experts were beginning to voice doubts concerning their value. More and more, military thinking was concerned with nuclear bombs and guided missiles.

POST-WORLD WAR II CARRIERS

Name	Number	Year Completed	Displacement (Tons)	Length of Flight Deck (Feet)
Midway	CV-41	1945	64,100	977
Franklin D. Roosevelt	CV-42	1945	64,100	977
Coral Sea	CV-43	1947	63,800	977
(Unnamed)	CV-44	(Cancelled)	—	—
(Unnamed)	CV-56	(Cancelled)	—	—
(Unnamed)	CV-57	(Cancelled)	—	—
Saipan	CVL-48	1946	18,700	684
Wright	CVL-49	1947	18,700	684

It was the Air Force's job to deliver nuclear bombs and guided missiles, not the Navy's. Did this mean that the aircraft carrier was going to become obsolete?

Not at all, said the Navy. The solution was simply to build carriers with flight decks long enough to launch the bigger, heavier planes that were capable of carrying nuclear bombs. The solution was the supercarrier.

U.S.S. *Midway*, pictured here in dry dock in San Francisco, was the first of post-World War II carriers.

The Air Force protested, saying that the Navy was getting involved in *its* mission.

For a time, it looked as if the Navy had won the argument. In July, 1948, construction of a new carrier, a carrier even bigger than those of the *Midway* class, was approved by Congress and President Harry Truman. The new vessel was to be named the *United States*.

But the *United States* was never built. Criticism of carriers and the whole concept of carrier warfare kept growing and growing. The keel for the *United States* was laid in April, 1949, but before the month was out,

U.S.S. *Franklin D. Roosevelt*, a second postwar carrier, cruising in the Mediterranean.

The *Coral Sea* enters dry dock in Long Beach, California.

Secretary of Defense Louis Johnson cancelled construction of the vessel. Johnson said it wasn't needed because it would simply duplicate the strategic role assigned to the Air Force.

But Johnson's decision was to be upset by an abrupt turn of events. On June 25, 1950, over 60,000 North Korean troops, spearheaded by more than 100 Russian-built tanks, invaded South Korea. Two days later, President Truman ordered General of the Army Douglas MacArthur to aid South Korea, and he assigned the U.S. Seventh Fleet to provide tactical support, since South Korean airfields were quickly overrun by the attack from the north. He also commanded the Fleet to aid in the protection of Taiwan.

On July 3 of that year, aircraft from the *Valley Forge,* steaming in the Yellow Sea, went into action, launching strikes on airfields, supply lines, and transportation facilities around Pyongyang, not far from Seoul, the Korean capital. Later, other carriers, both of the *Essex* and *Midway* class, were ordered into the area.

The air war during the Korean War differed sharply from the campaigns of World War II. Aircraft were used in a steady stream to pummel land targets. Flying hours were longer. Antiaircraft fire was heavier.

The Korean War dragged on until 1953, the year the armistice was signed, ending the fighting.

Because aircraft carriers were again able to demonstrate their value, a boom in carrier construction followed. In July, 1951, the Navy won permission to construct a vessel somewhat similar in design to the *United States,* the ship which had been cancelled two years before.

The new carrier was to be named the *Forrestal,* honoring James V. Forrestal, the first Secretary of Defense. In July, 1955, the ship was christened by the widow of the man for whom it had been named.

At 79,250 tons, the *Forrestal* (CV-59) was the biggest carrier ever built. (That designation had previously been held by the *Shinano,* a Japanese carrier commissioned in 1944 and rated at 68,000 tons. The *Shinano* had a very brief career, having been sunk in Japanese waters by an American submarine late in 1944, only ten days after the vessl had gone into service.)

The *Forrestal's* flight deck, at 1,039 feet, was nearly one-fifth of a mile long, more than twelve times the length of the deck that Gene Ely had used in making the first takeoff from a carrier.

The *Forrestal* flight deck was 259 feet wide. Overall, it provided more than four acres of space for landings and takeoffs.

The *Forrestal* was laced with 180 miles of piping and 260 miles of electrical cable. Its four five-bladed propellers could generate 200,000 horsepower, driving the *Forrestal* through the water at speeds in excess of 30 knots.

The *Forrestal* boasted *two* runways, one angling away from the other.

U.S.S. *Saratoga* (CV-60) is a carrier of the *Forrestal* class.

A crew of 4,200 manned the ship. More than 19,000 meals were served aboard each day.

The *Forrestal* was, indeed, a supercarrier.

Ultimately, the Navy was provided with the funds to build four supercarriers of the *Forrestal* class. The others were the *Saratoga* (CV-60), *Ranger* (CV-61), and *Independence* (CV-62).

The *Forrestal* was not only a notable vessel because of its size, but also by virtue of its design. It had an unusual flight deck, a deck that provided not one, but two runway systems, one runway angling away from the other. A plane could be landing on one runway at the same time another plane was taking off from the second runway.

Besides efficiency, the angled deck system made for greater safety. In the straight-deck, single runway system, planes were often stored on the forward portion of the runway. Except for the hangar deck, where space was limited, there was no other place to park them.

Suppose a plane was coming in for a landing and its tail hook failed to catch an arresting wire. The pilot was likely to suddenly find himself bearing down on the cluster of parked aircraft. The results were sometimes tragic.

To prevent an incoming plane from piling into aircraft stored on the deck, a crash barrier was erected. In the case of jet aircraft, the barrier took the form of a stout nylon net that stretched across the deck, and which was designed to grab the wings of the plane and brake it to a stop.

But the system was less than satisfactory. There were cases of pilots who crashed into the barrier with gun and rocket switches in an "on" position. At impact, a pilot might hit the switches accidentally, spraying death and destruction in every direction. Or an airplane might be airborne and strike the top of the barricade, in which case it could flip over into the parked aircraft.

As one carrier crewman put it, "When a pilot loses the hook, climbs the barrier, and winds up in the pack, he's often a gone pigeon—along with anybody else in the vicinity."

One of the *Forrestal's* F-8 Crusaders flies over the vessel.

The design of the *Forrestal* helped to eliminate this problem. The runway that ran parallel to the island could be used for storing aircraft, while the angled runway could be used for takeoffs and landings.

When an incoming pilot failed to hook an arresting cable, he simply applied power to gain altitude, and circled around to approach again.

The angled deck concept was developed by the British at the end of World War II. They marked off an angled runway on the deck of a carrier of conventional design, and operated twin-engine attack planes from it. Pilots liked the idea that they didn't have to worry about colliding with the ship's island as they made their landings.

The United States Navy later conducted similar tests aboard the *Antietam* and *Midway,* and met with great success. All carriers since the *Forrestal* have included a flight deck of angled runway design, and those carriers built earlier have had their flight decks modified so as to have one.

Another safety feature aboard the *Forrestal* and all subsequent carriers had to do with the landing system. Putting a plane down on a carrier deck had always been a big problem. The flight deck looked like a postage stamp to the incoming pilot. And it was a postage stamp in motion, constantly pitching and rolling.

The traditional method of landing a plane was based on human judgment, the judgment of a Landing Safety Officer, or LSO. The LSO was posted on a catwalk that bordered the flight deck. He was to the pilot's left as the plane approached. Using a pair of small paddles, about the size of Ping-Pong paddles, the LSO signaled landing instructions to the pilot.

The system worked successfully in a majority of cases. But even the most skilled of LSOs was a human being, and like any human, subject to lapses in concentration and judgment.

At night or in conditions of poor visibility, the system did not work very well. The LSO was sometimes unable to make a clear judgment as to the speed and approach angle of the incoming plane.

But a *Forrestal* pilot did not have to depend on an LSO. He had a mechanical means of judging his flight "down the hill" and onto the deck.

It was all done with mirrors; in fact, it was called "the mirror landing system."

The mirror landing system was based upon a shielded beam of light that was focused upon a polished

Mirror system provides visual flight path to flight deck.

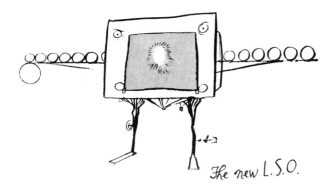

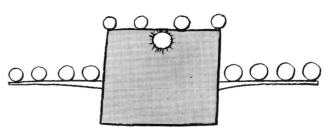

Above: Navy cartoon hailed the mirror system as "The New L.S.O."

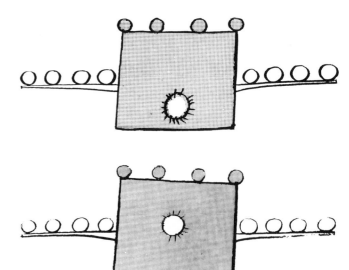

Right: If "meatball" edged above or below level of green lights, pilot adjusted his approach glide. Aim was to line up "meatball" with the lights (bottom picture).

aluminum mirror. The mirror was mounted at the spot where the LSO had been posted, to the left of the flight deck as the pilot made his approach. The mirror was tilted so as to bounce the beam into the air toward the aircraft, forming a visible glide path for the pilot.

All the pilot had to do was follow that reflected beam of light—or "meatball," as it was called—right down to the deck. If he did that, the wheels would touch down gently and his hook would engage an arresting wire.

The mirror looked like a giant television screen with an arm extending at right angles from each side. Each arm was strung with green lights, similar to traffic lights. These green lights were to assist the pilot in keeping the meatball precisely in the center of the mirror.

If the meatball slipped below the level of the green lights, the pilot knew his approach was too low. He'd better get more altitude or he might smack into the stern of the ship.

If the meatball was above the green lights, he knew he was too high, and likely to miss the arrester wires. Again, he'd adjust course.

The mirror landing system enabled the pilot to reduce his approach and touch-down to these three parts:

1. Airspeed
2. Lineup
3. Meatball

As the aircraft approached the flight deck, the pilot first checked to see that he was coming in at the proper airspeed. If his airspeed was right, he next checked to see that his plane was lined up with the centerline that was painted on the deck. Last, he got the meatball into the center of the mirror, and kept it there as he came in.

A pilot instruction manual of the 1950s put it in these terms: "If your airspeed is right, and you're on the centerline, you just follow the meatball home."

The mirror landing system could be used for any type of aircraft. In landing a propeller plane, a pilot would cut his throttle and flare the engines gently at the last second, whereas a jet had to come blazing in

It used to be   *like this . . .*

Mirror landing system reduced accidents and boosted pilot confidence in carrier operations.

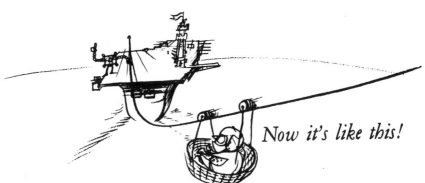

Now it's like this!

with all the power on, simply flying right into the wires. By tilting the mirror, the system could be made to accommodate either type of aircraft.

You can perform a simple experiment to demonstrate how the glide path could be varied by changing the mirror's tilt. Hold a flashlight in one hand and a hand mirror in the other, and shine the light onto the mirror, reflecting the beam onto a wall. By tilting the mirror forward or back, you adjust the angle of the reflected beam. With the mirror landing system, the mirror control officer did basically the same thing, except he used push buttons.

The mirror system took the horror out of night landings. The angled deck was lined on both sides with red boundary lights, like a runway at a land base. The runway's centerline was clearly outlined in white lights, which were flush with the deck. "You can spot the meatball from surprisingly far out," an instruction manual advised pilots. "The problem can be in keeping it from getting too bright."

Even if the weather was rough and the ship was pitching and rolling, the mirror system was stabilized to compensate, and the glide path remained normal.

Thanks to the mirror landing system and the angled runway, air operations aboard the *Forrestal* were rendered much less hazardous. Indeed, the *Forrestal* had an accident rate that was one-half that of the smaller, straight-deck *Essex*-class vessels.

Once a plane had touched down on the *Forrestal's* deck, its forward speed was braked by a cable arrester system that, in theory, at least, was not unlike the rope-and-sandbag arrangement that Gene Ely had used in making the very first carrier landing in 1910.

When the *Langley,* the first carrier, went into operation, it offered cross-deck wires that were connected to heavy weights that fitted into vertical shafts, something like the sash weights in a window frame. On landing, the plane's tail hook caught a wire, and the craft was yanked to a stop.

In addition to the cross-deck wires, a second set of wires, spaced about two feet apart, ran fore and aft just above the flight deck. These were meant to keep the plane from swerving to either the right or left as it landed. Both the *Lexington* and *Saratoga,* commissioned in 1927, five years after the *Langley,* had this type of landing system.

During the 1930s, the landing system went through a period of change. The fore-and-aft wires were replaced by a hydraulic system. As the plane set down on the deck and started to veer in one direction, a compensating mechanism would increase pressure in the other direction, which served to tug the plane toward the center of the deck.

And instead of weights at the opposite ends of the cross-deck wires, hydraulic "snubbers" went into use.

A snubber consisted of a piston that moved against the resistance of an oil-filled cylinder. This system, modified and improved through the years, is what is used today.

The number of cross-deck wires had been reduced to four by the time the *Forrestal* went into service. An incoming pilot would attempt to pass over the first two wires and get his plane's tail hook to engage wire No. 3. All carrier landings are graded, and catching the third wire would help the pilot to earn a high mark.

Flight operations aboard the *Forrestal* were also improved by installation of new, much more powerful steam catapults. And there were four catapults on the *Forrestal,* not just two.

How powerful were the *Forrestal*'s catapults? Consider this: For a land-based takeoff, a modern jet requires a mile-long air strip. But the *Forrestal*'s catapults could fling a jet into the air in just a few hundred feet.

It's not wrong to use the word "fling" in describing how a jet plane is launched from a carrier. The system works something like a slingshot, a Y-shaped stick with an elastic band fastened between the prongs of the Y. When you load the slingshot with a small pebble, draw the elastic back and release, you catapult the pebble away.

There's no elastic band involved in putting a carrier plane into the air, but there is a related part, a bridle, a heavy metal strap that connects the aircraft to the catapult shuttle. The shuttle is mounted into a metal slot that runs the length of the runway.

When a plane is about to be launched, the pilot guns the engine, building up power. But the aircraft doesn't go anywhere. A second metal strap, called a holdback, one end of which is fixed to the underbelly of the plane, the other end to the deck, prevents the plane from moving.

At this stage, the pilot is merely building up tension, the same as when the elastic band on a slingshot is drawn back.

When sufficient tension has been built, the catapult is fired. The plane breaks the grip of the holdback and surges down the deck and into the air.

In early carrier operations, catapult systems weren't looked upon as being really necessary. Aircraft were

Crewmen prepare an RA-5C Vigilante for launching.

As aircraft is about to be catapulted into the air, plane director supervises operations.

relatively light in weight at the time, so it didn't take an enormous amount of speed to get a plane into the air. The length of the flight deck was ample for most takeoffs.

What's said above held true even during the early months of World War II. An exception occurred in the case of the early escort carriers, discussed in the previous chapter.

Escort carriers were cargo vessels that had been converted to carrier use, then armed with aircraft equipped for antisubmarine warfare. They were used in escorting supply ships and tankers across the Atlantic Ocean.

Escort carriers were slow-moving vessels. They had a limited amount of deck space when compared to "real" carriers. What was even worse, the installation of the flight deck made these vessels top heavy. In anything but the calmest seas, they rolled and pitched in an alarming manner.

Catapults were an absolute necessity aboard such ships. Without them, air operations would have been limited to those rare days when wind and weather conditions were perfect. It was aboard these carriers that the first successful catapult systems were developed.

There are many advantages in using catapults. The chief benefit is that it increases the vessel's capability in delivering planes to the target area. Since much less deck space is needed for take-off operations, a greater number of aircraft can be arrayed on the deck for launching. Indeed, a catapult-equipped vessel can carry up to 40 percent more aircraft than one without a catapult system. It can also carry bigger aircraft, heavier aircraft.

And the catapult enables a vessel to launch aircraft at any time, at night as well as day, in virtually every type of weather. Night operations without the use of lights (as in wartime) can be carried out in routine fashion. On launching, the aircraft is sent away on a straight line; there's no need for the pilot to have to look to either his right or left in an effort to keep the plane on course.

Once the catapult accelerates the aircraft to safe flying speed, the pilot continues a normal climb, using instruments.

Rough weather is not a problem, either. Just as in night operations, the catapult assures a straight takeoff. Launches can be timed to the roll or pitch of the ship, with the aircraft fired away at the precise moment the deck's position is the most favorable.

Even strong crosswinds have little or no effect upon a launch. Before the use of catapults, it was necessary for a carrier to head into the prevailing wind during launch operations. The flow of air rushing over the deck assisted the plane in getting airborne.

Stout cable brakes the deck speed of A-6 Intruder.

An A-7A Corsair II is readied for launch aboard the U.S.S. *America* (CV-66).

But changing the carrier's course wasn't always practical. Indeed, it could be perilous. Suppose the task force happened to be steaming east, but the prevailing winds were coming out of the west. This would mean that the carrier would have to change direction by 180 degrees in order to launch aircraft. In other words, it would be steaming *away* from the ships assigned to protect it. But with catapults, carrier captains never had to face such a dilemma.

The surge in carrier construction that had been triggered by the Korean War continued through the 1960s, when five supercarriers were built—the *Kitty Hawk* (CV-63), *Constellation* (CV-64), *Enterprise* (CVN-65), *America* (CV-66), and *John F. Kennedy* (CV-67).

These vessels were slightly bigger versions of the *Forrestal.* One of them, the *Enterprise,* was special. Naval experts said the *Enterprise* signaled a new era in carrier development.

5/

"Underway on Nuclear Power"

A ship that runs on oil—a fossil-fuel ship, as it might be called—gets its power by burning oil that heats water in huge boilers. The heated water is converted to steam, and the steam is made to turn big turbines that are geared to the propeller drive shaft.

Nuclear-powered ships are driven by steam turbines, too. What the nuclear reactor does is provide the heat that generates the steam, that, in turn, drives the turbines.

The Navy began getting interested in nuclear propulsion in the 1940s. Nuclear reactors would be ideally suited for submarines, the Navy theorized.

The submarine is, by its very nature, an instrument that depends on stealth. It must conceal itself in the ocean depths almost indefinitely, then, unseen and unheard, must strike with great suddenness.

But submarines were not always able to perform in this fashion. In reality, they were merely surface ships which were capable of submerging for short periods of time.

The submarine's oil-fired engines made it necessary that large amounts of hull space be devoted to fuel storage. And since the subs depended on electric batteries for power, these vessels had to surface periodically in order to recharge their batteries.

Submarines of World War II could not stay submerged any longer than those in use a full three decades before. On patrol, a submarine might move as slowly as one knot when submerged to stretch the life of precious batteries. On some occasions, a sub might shut down its engines and just drift, hoping to squeeze out a bit more undersea time.

Naval officials realized that a nuclear submarine could overcome these disadvantages. It would never have to surface to recharge batteries. Combustion engines and the enormous fuel storage spaces they required would be eliminated. Such a vessel would truly be at home in the undersea world.

World War II ended in 1945, and the following year the Navy's Nuclear Power Division was reactivated under Admiral Hyman G. Rickover. Before the decade was over, a shipyard in Groton, Connecticut, where many World War II submarines had been built, was assigned to design and construct the first nuclear

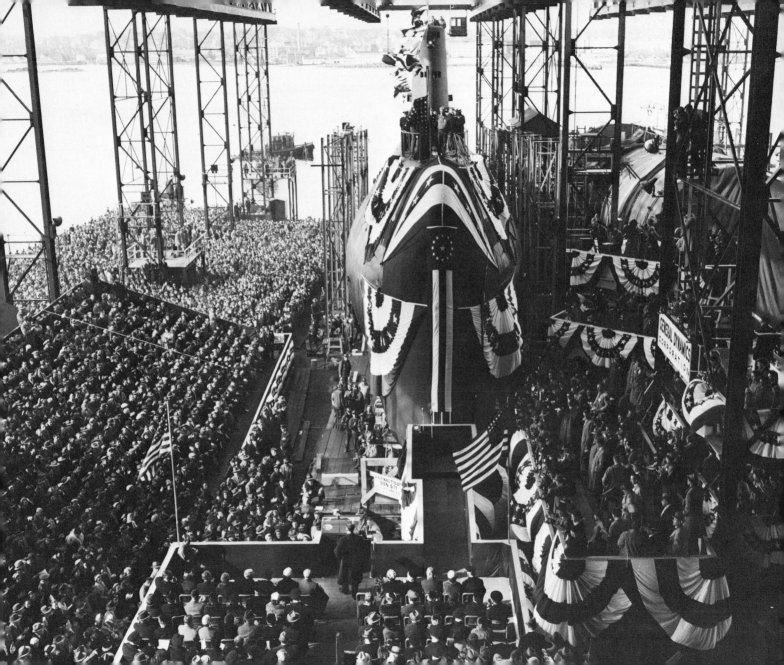

vessel. At the same time, at a secret location in Idaho, the first reactor that would power a ship was to be developed.

On a sunny day in 1952, at Groton, President Harry S. Truman signed the first hull plate of the ship that was to become the U.S.S. *Nautilus,* the first nuclear submarine. And a year and half later, Mrs. Dwight D. Eisenhower, the new President's wife, broke the traditional bottle of champagne over the bow of the *Nautilus.*

On January 17, 1955, the *Nautilus* went to sea for the first time. As it eased away from its pier on Connecticut's Thames River, the vessel flashed an historic message—"Underway on nuclear power."

The *Nautilus* was a success from the beginning. The vessel's first extended voyage, from New London, Connecticut, to San Juan, Puerto Rico—more than 1,300 miles in 84 hours, while submerged—enabled the *Nautilus* to break every existing submarine record for speed, endurance, and range.

One August 3, 1958, the *Nautilus* further dramatized its undersea capability by crossing *under* the North Pole. When the vessel returned to New York, its crew received a tumultuous welcome in New York City.

Steaming under the polar ice cap while submerged was really only the beginning for nuclear subs. In 1960, the *Triton,* powered by two nuclear reactors, followed the route of Ferdinand Magellan, and sailed around the world. Only the *Triton* did it submerged. It took 84 days.

During the 1960s, nuclear submarines went through a period of significant change. They stopped being boats; nuclear power enabled them to become ships, as they grew in size and weight by leaps and bounds.

At the same time the Navy was developing its nuclear submarine technology, nuclear surface ships were being planned. A nuclear-powered aircraft carrier would have several advantages over a fossil-fueled carrier.

An oil-burning carrier, such as the *Forrestal,* had to have enormous fuel storage spaces, enough to hold 8,500 tons of oil. But when operating at high speeds, the *Forrestal* used up as much as one-half of its fuel in just a few days.

Since the Navy wants its ships ready for any mission at a moment's notice, fuel tanks are not allowed to get less than half full. That means that the *Forrestal* and other carriers of that class must rendezvous with tankers every few days. Tankers, being slow-moving vessels, reduce the mobility of fighting ships. A

Nuclear-powered *Enterprise* **(CVN-65) with planes spotted on flight deck.**

Left: Superstructure of *Enterprise* is unlike that of any other Navy vessel.

Below: A view of the huge propellers of the *Enterprise.*

nuclear-powered carrier would never have to be "tied to the apron strings" of a tanker.

In addition, with a nuclear carrier, it would be easier to set up advance bases, because there would be no need to construct fuel storage facilities. Tankers and other ships necessary to the delicate task of transferring fuel at sea could be eliminated.

On February 4, 1958, the keel for the first nuclear supercarrier was laid at the naval shipyard at Newport News, Virginia. The vessel was commissioned as the *Enterprise* in November, 1961, and given the designation CVN-65, the N standing for nuclear.

The *Enterprise* was not the first nuclear-powered surface ship. That billing goes to a merchant vessel, the *Savannah,* launched in 1959.

Built at a cost of $40 million, the sleek *Savannah* carried some cargo and passengers, but mostly it was used for showing off. Between 1959 and 1962, the vessel traveled 130,000 miles, visiting forty ports, in demonstrating that an "atomic ship," as it was sometimes called in those days, could be operated safely. More than 1.5 million people visited the *Savannah* on its stops in foreign ports.

While the ship did prove to be safe, it was also expensive, costing the federal government about $3 million a year to keep in operation. This was judged too much to pay for a ship whose purpose was mostly ornamental, and in 1971 the *Savannah* was taken out of service.

At the time the *Enterprise* was commissioned, it ranked, at 85,000 tons, as the largest warship ever built. The ship's flight deck was 1,040 feet in length and 252 feet wide.

Any one of its four powerful catapults could accelerate a plane weighing as much as 78,000 pounds to a speed of 160 miles per hour in a distance of only 250 feet. When all of its catapults were in use, the *Enterprise* could launch aircraft at the rate of one every 15 seconds.

The *Enterprise* surpassed the Navy's highest hopes. For three years, beginning in November, 1961, the vessel steamed 207,000 miles, the equivalent of more than eight trips around the world at the equator, and the ship's eight nuclear reactors never needed refueling once.

Of course, it was still necessary to meet tankers at sea to take on jet fuel for the aircraft. But because the *Enterprise* didn't have to carry 8,500 tons of fuel, as the *Forrestal* did, more storage space could be given over to aviation fuel.

There were other advantages, too. When a ship burns oil, corrosive fumes are generated, which are exhausted up the stacks. These gases eat away at sensitive radar and radio equipment, fixed high on the masts directly in the path of the fumes.

Soot, also generated by a fossil-fuel ship, is another problem, a maintenance problem. It settles everywhere. At least twice a day, deck crews have to hose down areas exposed to soot fallout. But with a nuclear vessel, there is no soot and no stack gases.

The heated exhaust gases also cause an area of low pressure over the carrier flight deck. This makes for a slight turbulence that incoming planes encounter. Pilots call it "ramp burble."

When a plane passes through this area of turbulence, it has about the same effect as when an automobile strikes a pothole. It doesn't cause an accident; it doesn't do any damage. It just jolts the man at the wheel and the passengers. Nuclear power eliminated such jolts.

What is it like to live aboard a ship with eight nuclear reactors? Nobody seems to notice their presence.

During the periods the nuclear power plant is being operated, high levels of radiation exist around the reactor. In addition, the fluids flowing through the reactor are said to be "active" and capable of giving off harmful radiation.

To protect personnel aboard the ship, heavy shielding is required around the reactor. Concrete, lead, water, plastics, and steel are used as shielding materials.

In addition, radiation monitoring systems are employed throughout the ship. These keep a check on the purity of air being circulated.

Specially trained personnel also conduct daily "swipe tests." In these, random spots on decks, bulkheads, and overheads are wiped down with small paper discs. The particles collected on the discs are then analyzed for possible radiation.

Each crewman whose duties take him anywhere near the reactor must wear a small glass cylinder on his belt, called a dosimeter. The dosimeter measures the amount of radiation to which the crew member has been exposed.

Provisions are also made for the safe storage of the reactor's liquid and gaseous wastes. Sealed tanks are

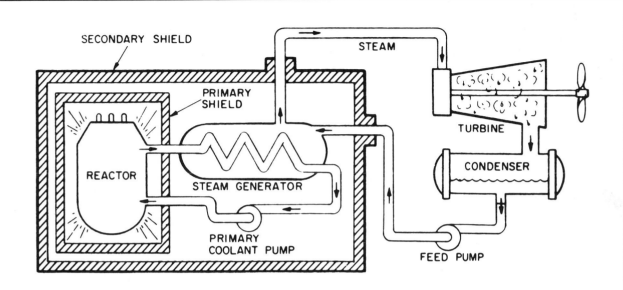

SECONDARY SHIELD

STEAM

PRIMARY SHIELD

REACTOR

STEAM GENERATOR

PRIMARY COOLANT PUMP

TURBINE

CONDENSER

FEED PUMP

HOW NUCLEAR ENERGY POWERS A SHIP

The power plant of a nuclear ship is based upon a nuclear reactor that provides the heat necessary to generate steam. The steam is fed into the turbines that drive the ship's propellers.

After passing through the turbines, the steam is condensed. The water that results is piped back to the steam generators by feed pumps.

The heated water from which the steam is derived is pressurized to prevent boiling. After it leaves the steam generator, it is fed into coolant pumps, and then back into the reactor for reheating.

Above: Dosimeter, worn at the belt, measures radiation levels.

Right: Nuclear-powered guided missile cruiser *Long Beach* rolls with the waves off Cape Horn.

Opposite page: The *Bainbridge,* a guided missile frigate, is also nuclear-powered.

provided for liquid wastes. Gaseous wastes are stored in heavy containment vessels or absorbed by charcoal, which is then stored in sealed containers.

Several other nuclear-powered surface ships went into service in the 1960s, including the *Long Beach,* a guided missile cruiser, and the *Bainbridge,* a guided missile frigate. On May 13, 1964, the *Enterprise* joined these two vessels to form the world's first nuclear-powered task force.

To demonstrate its speed and mobility, the task force made a 65-day, globe-circling voyage, without once receiving fuel, food, or provisions of any type. Operation Sea Orbit, it was called.

In January of the following year, 1965, the *Enterprise* and other ships of the Navy stopped playing games.

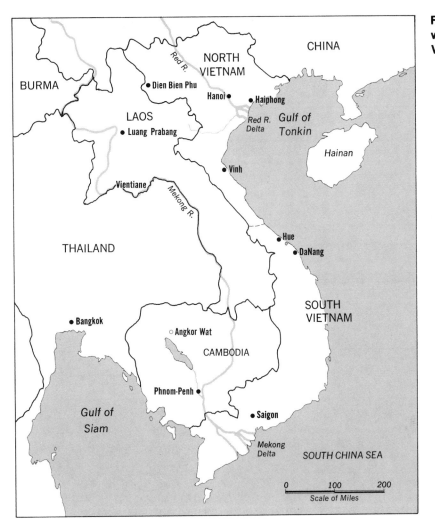

From 1954 until 1976, Vietnam was divided into North Vietnam and South Vietnam.

CHINA

NORTH VIETNAM

BURMA

• Dien Bien Phu

Red R.

Hanoi • • Haiphong

LAOS

Red R. Delta

Gulf of Tonkin

• Luang Prabang

Hainan

• Vinh

Vientiane

Mekong R.

THAILAND

• Hue

• DaNang

SOUTH VIETNAM

• Bangkok

○ Angkor Wat

CAMBODIA

Phnom-Penh •

Gulf of Siam

• Saigon

Mekong Delta

SOUTH CHINA SEA

0   100   200

Scale of Miles

A-POWERED 'BIG E' IN THE WAR

Launches 140 Jets

THE ENTERPRISE, MOST POWERFUL SHIP AFLOAT, AT SEA   Thurs., Dec. 2, 1965   New York Journal-American

Big headlines hailed arrival of *Enterprise* in waters off Vietnam.

The United States was becoming deeply involved in Vietnam. Carriers were to play a major role there for the next decade.

United States interest in Vietnam has been traced to 1950 when President Harry Truman sent a 35-man American advisory team to the area. That interest continued through the administrations of Presidents Dwight D. Eisenhower, John F. Kennedy, Lyndon B. Johnson, and Richard M. Nixon.

The major American involvement began in August, 1964, when a pair of United States destroyers was reportedly attacked by North Vietnamese torpedo boats in the Gulf of Tonkin. Not long after, Congress gave President Johnson the power "to take all necessary measures to repel any armed attack against the forces of the United States, and prevent further aggression."

In February, 1965, the President ordered continuous bombing raids over Vietnam. At the time, airfields

95

Above: Carrier pilot from U.S.S. _Hancock_ describes air action over Vietnam during debriefing.

Below: North Vietnamese bridge was early victim to American carrier-based bombers.

PHUONG CAN HWY BR
9 APRIL 1965

ONE SPAN DROPPED

HOANG MAI

in the South were not equipped to handle powerful jet aircraft. Carriers in the western Pacific were ordered into position.

Throughout much of the war, which was to last until 1975, when peace pacts were signed and the last Americans evacuated, the Navy kept five aircraft carriers committed to duty in the Pacific, and three were constantly in service off the coast of Vietnam. The *Enterprise* reached the area late in November, 1965, and took up a position near Saigon, then the capital.

On December 2, the *Enterprise* became the first nuclear-powered ship in history to enter combat, launching air strikes against targets in the South. *Enterprise* planes flew 137 sorties that day, destroying a bridge, a communications station, and 92 other structures. *Enterprise* planes also sank two sampans.

On a typical day for the *Enterprise,* wave after wave of planes would roar from the ship—droop-nosed Phantom bombers, chunky Whales, used as airborne tankers, two-engine Intruders, stuffed with computers and other electronic gear that enabled the plane to bomb in any kind of weather, and small, swift Skyhawks, whose pilots called them "Tinkertoys."

"A pilot gets up," a commander said, "eats his breakfast and gets into his flight gear. He then reports to the ready room two hours before launch time, for a briefing. The hop usually lasts about two hours. This is followed by a debriefing. This can last from 30 minutes to an hour. Then he eats, rests, and the cycle begins all over again."

In the ready room, a squadron commander briefed his men: "OK, the code word for MIGs [enemy jets] today is 'porkchop.' If you spot anything, sing out and go after him. Whatever you do, don't try to take those Skyhawks through rain squalls. They're not built for it."

As the commander spoke, the first planes were being launched, and the scream of jet engines could be heard overhead. The pilots in the ready room began climbing into their bulky survival vests and donning their oxygen masks. It was 15 minutes to flight time.

On this day, Lieutenant Commander Eugene McDaniel, an Intruder pilot, hit a string of boxcars in the town of Quinvanh. Huge fireballs billowed up from five of them. Other pilots said the area was still covered with thick gray smoke hours later.

The Phantoms bombed a barge loading area not far from Thanhoa, as well as several beached barges

An A-4 Skyhawk (foreground) is prepared for launch aboard the *Enterprise,* as an F-4 Phantom thunders overhead.

south of Navinh. The Skyhawks peppered enemy infiltration routes in the mountains southwest of Donghoi.

But none of the planes did very much damage. The weather was too foul for anything more than "nibbling at the edges," as one pilot put it. There was no antiaircraft fire and no enemy planes were encountered.

There were days when the antiaircraft fire was fearsome, however. "You have to fly through a haze of tracer fire first," one pilot said, "with flak bursting all around you. Sometimes it seems like everyone and his brother has an automatic rifle and is shooting at you.

Ordnancemen aboard the _Enterprise_ arm an F-4 Phantom in preparation for a combat mission over Vietnam.

An A-4 Skyhawk returns to the *Enterprise* after mission over Vietnam.

"We expected antiaircraft fire to be heavy over here, but not this heavy. And just one little bullet can knock a million dollar aircraft out of the sky."

Sometimes targets are "inside the SAM envelope," which means that the attacking aircraft are within easy range of enemy surface-to-air-missiles, given to the North Vietnamese by the Soviet Union. SAMs were not accurate below 1,500 feet, however, so pilots sighting SAMs would dive low. But that strategy meant running a far greater risk of being hit by antiaircraft fire.

Those men who worked on the flight deck—purple-shirted fuelers, red-shirted ordnance handlers, and blue-shirted plane pushers—sometimes worked 18 hours a day, getting sleep on the wings of planes to which they had been assigned.

In mid-1967, the *Enterprise* returned to the United States, the ship's combat responsibilities being taken over by another carrier. At the Alameda (California) Naval Air Station, the ship was fitted out with the Sea Sparrow, a defensive missile system.

At the time, the *Enterprise*'s primary defense was its F-4 Phantoms. The carrier also operated with escort ships that carried long-range missiles.

The Sea Sparrow launchers provided a last-ditch defense. When the *Enterprise* radar picked up hostile aircraft or missiles eight miles away, two or more missiles would be fired in succession. The missiles raced for their targets at four times the speed of sound.

Navy officials applauded the performance of carriers, in general, and the *Enterprise*, in particular, in Vietnam. "It's almost corny," said the ship's commander, Captain James L. Holloway, "but I think 'magnificent' is the only word that can be used to describe the *Enterprise*'s action in combat."

Other naval officials were just as lavish in their praise.

Aircraft carriers had demonstrated their worth once more. Vietnam land bases had been limited in what they could do and were vulnerable to attack. It had been easy to put carriers into position. They were already in the western Pacific, ready to go.

The Vietnam experience would be used by the Navy as an argument for building more carriers. Other Vietnams are at least as likely to develop as a nuclear war against the Soviet Union, Navy strategists said. So having the mobility and striking power that carriers offer was at least as important as having bombers and intercontinental missiles.

6/

Triple-Threat Carriers

During the 1970s, the Navy faced two tough problems:

- The size of its carrier force was dwindling, as old World War II carriers had to be retired.
- The Soviet Navy kept getting bigger; thus, the Soviet's capability in controlling the seas kept increasing.

To get as much value as possible out of the carriers then in service, the Navy decided to make each a multimission carrier.

Navy aircraft were originally used only for observation and scouting. During World War II, carrier planes were first used as long-range artillery, but with the added advantage that they could be "fired" from a mobile platform.

Also during World War II, fighters and torpedo planes from carriers were used to combat the submarine menace. And, of course, its aircraft played a vital role in the defense of the carrier.

The modern aircraft carrier has the ability to perform any or all of these missions, thanks to the wide variety of aircraft deployed aboard it.

Some of its aircraft are attack aircraft. Their role is to pound enemy forces on the land or sea.

Mix of aircraft aboard _Nimitz_ includes F-4J Phantom, E-2B Hawkeye, A-6 Intruder, and A-7 Corsair II.

F-14 Tomcat sets down on flight deck of U.S.S. *Ranger* (CV-61).

Other aircraft have a defensive role. They detect and identify enemy aircraft; they knock them out of the sky.

Still others are antisubmarine aircraft. They are equipped to detect and destroy enemy submarines.

Such carriers are called "triple-threat" carriers. The triple-threat concept was first tried out aboard the *Saratoga* during the ship's Mediterranean cruise in 1971. Before the ship left its home port, special detection equipment used in antisubmarine warfare had to be installed aboard. Additional ready rooms had to be provided for the squadrons of pilots who were to fly antisubmarine missions. Finally, aircraft of several different types had to be deployed aboard.

The *Saratoga* passed all of its tests successfully. When the ship returned to the United States from the Mediterranean, it ranked as the Navy's first multimission carrier.

All carriers today are triple-threat carriers. Take, for example, the U.S.S. *Nimitz,* a nuclear-powered supercarrier that joined the fleet in 1975. It is capable of carrying 100 airplanes. They can be of at least eight different types:

F-14 TOMCAT—One of the Navy's newest fighter-interceptors, the Tomcat is a two-engine aircraft that is capable of flying at twice the speed of sound. Its sophisticated electronics gear permits the plane to operate in even the worst of flying weather. A unique feature of the Tomcat is its variable sweep wing, which gives the plane great maneuverability. The Tomcat is armed with three types of missiles: the Sparrow, Sidewinder, and long-range Phoenix.

A-7 CORSAIR II—This single-engine jet acts as either a strike bomber or is used in support of a ground attack. Manned by a single pilot, the Corsair II can carry air-to-air missiles, air-to-ground missiles, or general purpose bombs. Its armament includes a 20-mm cannon. The Corsair uses an advanced computer system for both weapons delivery and navigation.

A-6 INTRUDER—A two-man attack plane, the two-engine Intruder is capable of delivering several different types of projectiles to the assigned target. It can carry five 2,000-pound bombs or as many as 24

Pilots man an A-7 Corsair II and an A-6 Intruder aboard the *Nimitz*.

Above: Ordnance crewman arms an A-7 Corsair II.

Right: A-7 Corsair circles before landing on U.S.S. *Saratoga* (CV-60) flight deck.

500-pound bombs. The plane's electronics equipment enables it to drop its payload on targets that are completely obscured by thick clouds or darkness. A modified version of the Intruder (the KA-6D) serves as a tanker plane for in-flight refueling.

An A-6 Intruder is readied for launch.

Side view of A-6 Intruder shows wing's fold-back feature.

An EA-6B Prowler approaches the flight deck of the *Enterprise*.

EA-6B PROWLER—Designed for tactical use in electronic warfare, the Prowler is a two-engine, four-seat turbojet which has a flying speed of more than 500 knots. It is laden with complex electronic systems, including sensitive receivers and powerful jammers that are meant to deny enemy forces the use of their radar and radio equipment. The Prowler is the most expensive, if not *the* most expensive, of all the aircraft aboard the *Nimitz*.

S-3A VIKING—A two-engine jet that carries a crew of four and boasts an endurance time of more than seven hours, the Viking is the newest of the Navy's antisubmarine warfare aircraft. It carries surface and subsurface search equipment, including advanced radar and sonar systems. It is also equipped with

An S-3A Viking, assigned to the *John F. Kennedy,* in flight off San Diego.

Here an S-3A Viking is launched from the flight deck of the *Kitty Hawk*.

metal-detecting equipment that is based on the measurement of magnetic intensities. As the Viking gathers data, its computer processes, interprets, and stores it. The airplane is used chiefly for search missions in the vicinity of the carrier task force.

110

RA-5C VIGILANTE—Reconnaissance is the Vigilante's mission. A two-seat, twin-engine aircraft, it has been fitted out with the latest photographic equipment. It is capable of photographing and collecting intelligence information while breezing along at more than twice the speed of sound. Needle-nosed and sleek, the Vigilante has an overall length of 75 feet, 10 inches, making it the longest aircraft on board the carrier.

An RA-5C Vigilante comes in for recovery on the *Independence.*

E-2B HAWKEYE—Its distinctive rotating radar dome (which houses its radar antenna) is the tip-off that this airplane is an information gatherer. Besides radar, the Hawkeye carries specialized communications and computer equipment. The aircraft is used to control carrier air traffic, provide area surveillance, and assist search-and-rescue missions. It also plays a role as a communications relay station.

The Hawkeye is powered by two Allison turboprop engines, which drive two four-blade, full-feathering, constant-speed propellers. The engines have earned the Hawkeye another nickname: the Hummer.

E-2B Hawkeye's distinctive dome houses radar antenna. Scene is aboard the _Enterprise_.

Navy's SH-3D Sea King has a workhorse role.

SH-3H Sᴇᴀ Kɪɴɢ—When based aboard aircraft carriers, helicopters have a workhorse role, and the Sea King is typical. It is used in antisubmarine warfare missions, provides rescue and assistance in the case of ditched aircraft or in "man overboard" situations, and is also used in transferring cargo and personnel from one vessel to another at sea.

The Sea King is a gas turbine craft, capable of staying airborne for more than five hours at a time. It is equipped with sonar and magnetic detection equipment, and also multichannel relay equipment to report whatever it finds.

The *Nimitz,* like any other carrier, can emphasize one of its roles over another by changing the mix of aircraft it carries. If ranging into an area where enemy submarines are known to lurk, the carrier can take on more than the usual number of ASW aircraft. Should the *Nimitz* be assigned to launch an assault, an added number of attack aircraft would be provided. No matter the mission it is assigned, the *Nimitz* can adjust for it.

7/

Men Who Man the Nimitz

Although a supercarrier such as the *Nimitz* contains a complex assortment of sophisticated aircraft and weapons, the Navy fully realizes that the vessel gets its driving force from its men. They have to be thoroughly trained. They have to be willing to work hard. This chapter profiles a representative handful of the *Nimitz*'s 5,600 crew members.

In days past, a typical sailor was a well-muscled seaman. He was skilled in heaving lines, tying knots, and handling small boats.

That's changed. Ships today are awash with automated equipment and electronic gadgetry. Men are still needed to do deck work, but the typical Navy man is likely to be a technical specialist, spending his working hours listening to sonar equipment or watching a radarscope.

When a man enters the Navy, it is almost certain that he lacks in skill and experience. "Most of the men aboard this ship," says Commander R.L. Leuschner, executive officer of the *Nimitz,* "had never even seen a carrier before they arrived aboard this one. They had never seen a jet fighter or a bomber."

As this suggests, the Navy has to go to great lengths to train recruits. Each man's skills and interests are first identified through a series of classification tests. He then decides upon an occupational field.

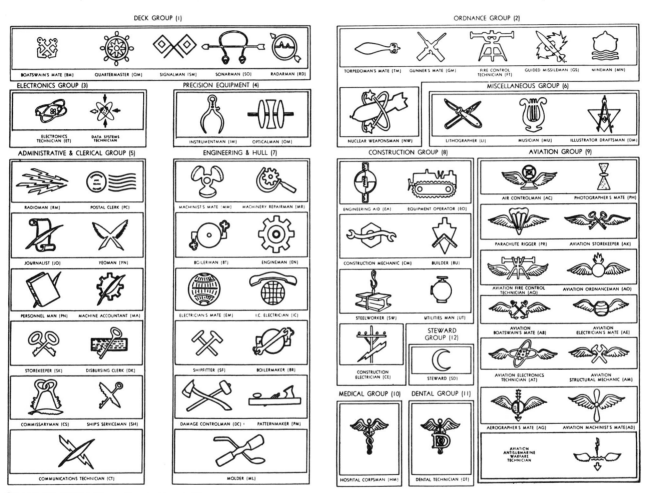

Specialty marks for various occupations.

There are dozens of occupations from which to choose. They're called ratings. Each has its own specialty mark or symbol.

After completing boot camp, or basic training, where he's introduced to naval customs and discipline, the recruit is likely to attend a service school. There he is taught the basic skills of the occupational field he's chosen. Later, aboard ship or at a shore station, the recruit gets "on-the-job" training.

Self-study is also part of the program. Personnel can select correspondence courses from an enormous array the Navy offers. Each course includes a textbook, a study guide, test material (there's a final exam at the end of each course), and even a supply of envelopes and paper.

Most recruits enlist for a three-year tour of duty. After that, a man has to decide whether to sign up for three more years or return to civilian life. It's usually not an easy decision.

The *Nimitz,* incidentally, is an all-male society. While there are about 25,000 women wearing Navy uniforms, only a small number has been assigned to duty aboard ships, and none serve aboard warships. "This is going to change," says Commander Leuschner. "Women represent a vast talent pool we hope to be able to draw upon one day soon. We not only want women, we *need* them."

Tall, dark Joe Melnick, from the Bronx, New York, was twenty years old when he joined the Navy. After he graduated from high school, Joe had planned to continue his education, and started attending Iona College in New Rochelle, New York, not far from his home in the Bronx. "But I had some problems," Joe recalls, "a few problems at home, and some problems with my girlfriend.

"Then the car I was using to get to college broke down, and I couldn't get it fixed. So I started riding my bicycle to school.

"Then next thing that happened was that someone stole my bike. Everything was going wrong at once."

Joe quit college and decided to go to work, but he couldn't find a job. It was at this point that he started to think about joining one of the military services. A cousin of Joe's, who was already in the Navy, told him about the many training programs the Navy offered. Joe signed up.

Joe was sent to Orlando, Florida, for nine weeks of recruit training. During that time, he decided he would like to become a specialist in avionics, the science and technology of electrical and electronic devices used in aviation.

Being a graduate of the Bronx High School of Science was an asset. "I had done OK in high school," Joe says. "I graduated with an 82 average, and I had taken courses in electricity and physics."

After he completed boot camp, Joe was assigned to a Navy school in Memphis, Tennessee. There he was taught some of the basics of electricity and electronics. The school lasted three weeks.

By now, Joe had decided upon a particular rating, that of aviation fire controlman. That meant that during his career, Joe would be involved with the repair and maintenance of sophisticated electronic equipment—various types of radar and computers, guided missile equipment, and bomb direction

Joe Melnick—"When you're out at sea, the hours are long. You work a 12-hour day."

systems. After Memphis, Joe was sent to another school in Norfolk, which lasted three months and introduced him to these topics.

More advanced training followed, with Joe attending a third school, also in Norfolk, where he learned how to apply the knowledge and skills he had acquired. "They got deeper into everything," he recalls. "I worked with systems that simulated those on different aircraft. Plus there was classroom training."

Afterward, Joe was sent to a fourth school at Oceana, Virginia, not far from Norfolk. Here he was trained in the repair of a specific electronic system, the radar of the F-14.

When he had finished his schooling at Oceana, Joe had been in the Navy almost a full year, yet he had never even stepped aboard a ship. Almost all his time was school time.

But now his schooling was finished, at least for the present, and Joe was assigned to the *Nimitz*. "I started working right away," he recalls.

The shop that Joe works in is fitted out on all sides with test benches. Each bench is a tall stack of expensive electronic equipment, including a small screen, similar to the screen on a television set, on which test results are monitored.

When test and repair work is being done, the loud roar of air-conditioning equipment is constant. "You have to keep it cool in here," Joe says. "Otherwise, you'll have trouble with the electronic circuits. They could even burn out."

But the loudest noise comes from the aircraft. The flight deck is right above Joe's shop, and when a plane approaches the ship, you hear its engine screaming. It keeps getting louder and louder, ending in a tremendous crashing sound as the plane slams down onto the deck. It's the type of sound that might come from two cars colliding at high speeds. Joe scarcely notices it.

To get an idea of what Joe does, imagine the television set in your home to be made up of different removable components—one for the volume control, another for the tuner, another for the channel selector, and a fourth for the system that regulates picture brightness.

Suppose the set wasn't working properly. If it had been reduced to these components, you wouldn't have to send it out for repairs or call in a serviceman. All you would have to do is identify where the trouble was located. For example, if you couldn't tune the set properly, you'd know the tuner was broken. Then all

Joe fits a "black box" into his bench for testing.

you'd have to do is remove the tuner component and send it to the repair shop. Or you could simply buy a new tuner and install it in place of the old one.

Sophisticated aviation electronics systems are put together in somewhat the same fashion. Take the radar system of the F-14, the one in which Joe Melnick specializes. It is made up of approximately 20 major components, each of which is housed in a different black box. Some of these boxes are the size of cigar boxes; others are almost as big as milk crates.

When an F-14 pilot notices his radar isn't working right, the trouble is traced to a particular black box. The box is removed from the aircraft, and one that's working properly is installed in its place.

The problem box, along with a gripe sheet explaining how the system is misbehaving, is sent to the repair shop where Joe works. The gripe sheet gives Joe certain clues as to what's wrong with the box.

He begins testing the box on a special bench, putting electronic signals into it. The signals simulate the operating conditions of the box when it is aboard the aircraft. For each signal he injects into the box, Joe gets a reading on his test equipment.

Inside the box are a number of cards, each with an electronic circuit printed on it. Joe tries to isolate the problem to one of the printed circuits. Once he's been able to do this, it's simply a matter of replacing the faulty circuit with a good one. Then the box can be put back into service.

Sometimes Joe can find the problem circuit card within a matter of minutes. Other times, it may take him three or four hours.

"I enjoy what I'm doing," Joe says. "I've always been interested in electronics. I like the work.

"But when you're out at sea, the hours are long. You work a 12-hour day. You work seven days a week.

"You don't mind working, though, because there's not much else to do. It's easy to get bored; you can go a little crazy, in fact.

"Sometimes I go to the library when I have time off," Joe continues. "Or I go to the gym and work out. Other times, I'll just watch a movie on the ship's closed-circuit television. I play cards, usually canasta or pinochle. I play darts."

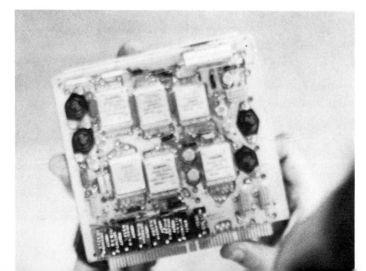

The "black box" contains printed circuit cards like this.

Some boxes—such as this one—contain about two dozen cards.

Joe is undecided about his future. He knows that if he remains in the Navy, he's likely to continue to do the same type of work he's doing today. He'll get additional training, go to more schools, that is, and learn to handle other types of radar and other types of electronic equipment. He'll advance in rating and get increases in pay. "A normal Navy career," he says.

But the civilian world seems attractive to him. Because of all the schooling he's received, Joe now has skills that are much in demand. "There are lots of possibilities out there," he says. "I could probably go to work for any one of the major electronics companies—IBM, Texas Instruments, or Hughes Aircraft.

"Take Hughes Aircraft, for instance. They make the equipment I work on. I could probably go to work for Hughes as a technical representative, doing the same work I'm doing now. Only I'd be making more money, a lot more.

"I have another year before I have to make up my mind. Then we'll see."

While the *Nimitz* is powered by two nuclear reactors, it also has a pair of huge diesel engines. These are standby engines, meant to operate should the nuclear system have to be shut down for any reason.

The diesel equipment has to be kept in a state of readiness, so if a switchover is necessary, it can be made

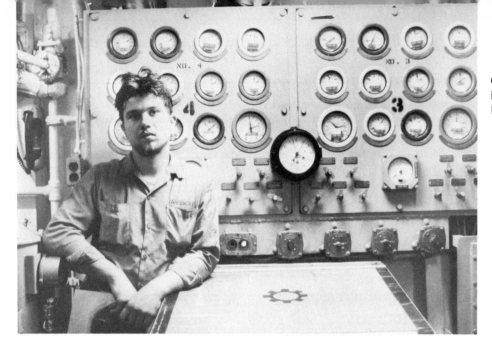

at a moment's notice. Keeping that equipment in first-class operating condition is one of the duties of twenty-one-year-old Chris Carpenter, an engineman first class.

When he's on watch—that is, on duty—Chris has to be sure that the diesel engines are in "auto-start condition," ready to pick up the power load should the nuclear equipment fail. "There are certain valves I have to check," Chris says, "and these valves have to be open at all times. I also have gauges to check; they must have certain readings at all times. I have to check the oil in the engines and make sure there's enough."

Besides his responsibilities as far as the diesel engines are concerned, Chris also has to help keep the *Nimitz*'s lifeboat engines and liberty boat engines in operating condition. (When the *Nimitz* anchors near a port city, a liberty boat is one that takes crew members on shore leave.)

If a liberty boat's engine breaks down, Chris has to get it operating again. And he has to do it quickly. "When we pull into a port and drop anchor, we've got 6,000 guys who are trying to get off the ship," Chris says, "and they're all trying to get off at the same time. We've got 12 liberty boats and they've all got to be running."

Chris comes from Wauchula, Florida. Before he joined the Navy, he traveled with his parents who operated carnival rides. They taught Chris how to run the ride machinery. At the time he entered the Navy, Chris could operate a Ferris wheel, a merry-go-round, and such rides as "The Scrambler," "The Twister," "The Bullet," and "The Rock-O-Plane." "Just about any kind of carnival ride," he says.

One important reason Chris joined the Navy was to get additional training in diesel mechanics and auto mechanics. He signed up for three years. "I want to be a diesel technician by the time I get out of the Navy," he says. He's looking forward to attending Navy schools that will instruct him in the operation, repair, and maintenance of sophisticated diesel equipment.

Chris has no interest in remaining in the Navy. "The Navy is fine for some people," he says. "But I'm not cut out for it.

"I like to be my own boss. I have my own way of doing things. I don't think too highly of having people telling me what to do. But in the Navy you have to do things the Navy way, and that's the only way you can do it."

Chris checks the engine on a liberty boat.

While Chris Carpenter and Joe Melnick spend most of their working hours below decks, twenty-year-old Sean Hardwick is one of the many hundreds of *Nimitz* crew members who works in the open air, up on the flight deck. Sean is what is called a "hook-up P.O. [petty officer]," and, as such, is in charge of hooking up about-to-be-launched aircraft to the catapult shuttle.

Sean's control station is a "bubble," a small, glass-walled communications center built into the flight deck. It moves up and down like an elevator. When a plane is about to be launched, the bubble descends into the deck until its top is flush with the deck. Seated inside the bubble, Sean has all of the launch controls at his fingertips.

The *Nimitz* was the first aircraft carrier to be equipped with a bubble system. On other carriers, flight officers standing on the deck use hand signals in giving orders to the catapult operator.

The second youngest of six children, Sean was born and brought up in White Hall, Illinois—what he calls "a really small town." Located forty miles north of St. Louis, White Hall is a farming community of about 3,000.

Sean went to high school in White Hall. He says he was an "average student," and that he probably could have done better. "I really didn't try at the time," he says. He liked sports, and played football and was a member of the track team. He also joined the school choral group.

Shortly after graduation, when he was seventeen, Sean signed up with the Navy. Why did he join? "I guess I just wanted to get away for a while," he says. "I'm the kind of person who likes to go different places and see if things are any better."

Right after he joined, the Navy sent Sean to the Great Lakes Naval Training Center for recruit training. "I wasn't sure what I really wanted at first," Sean says. "So after boot camp, I didn't choose any Navy schools to go to. I just wanted to look around and see what things were like."

The Navy assigned Sean to the *Nimitz*. Since he didn't have any training, he was given a menial job, that of ladling out food in one of the many dining rooms—or mess halls—aboard the ship. In Navy lingo, Sean was a messman.

"All of the time I was working in the mess hall," Sean recalls, "I used to go up onto the flight deck whenever I had time and watch what was going on." Sean thought that it would be exciting to be a member

Sean Hardwick—"It's exciting up
on the deck. I know it's something
I'll never experience again in my
life."

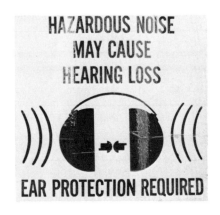

For those who work on the flight deck, jet noise is a constant hazard.

of a launch crew, and so he applied for a transfer. After several weeks of waiting, his request was granted, and he was assigned to operations at Catapult No. 1—"Cat 1," for short.

After some preliminary training, Sean was made a member of the crew that hooked up the holdback cable on each plane being launched. The holdback prevents the plane from rocketing off the deck until the catapult is actually fired.

One end of the holdback is attached to the deck, and the other end to a device called a tension bar that is fixed to the underside of the aircraft. The tension bar is about six inches long and shaped like an exercise dumbbell. The bar portion of the device snaps in two from the force generated by the firing of the catapult. Once free of the holdback's restraint, the plane hurtles down the deck and into the air.

Hooking up the holdback is not a job for the faint-hearted. It means scurrying out onto the deck amidst aircraft that are being launched and recovered, and then scampering under the designated plane and securing the cable end to the tension bar.

It is something like being asked to play in heavy traffic. There is the constant thunder of jet engines. Everyone on deck must wear a set of heavy earpieces to prevent inner ear damage. In Navy jargon, incidentally, an earpiece is called a "Mickey Mouse," since it makes the wearer look like he's donned a pair of big Mickey Mouse-type ears.

Crewmen attach a holdback cable in preparing a jet for launch.

Not only do the jet engines generate ear-splitting noise, but also suffocating heat, which boils about the deck in great clouds. The hot exhaust fumes can sear a person's skin in the blink of an eye. In moving about the deck, you learn never to pass behind an airplane; you go underneath it, instead.

Your senses are assaulted by exhaust fumes. Your nose twitches, your eyes water, and when you leave the flight deck and go below, you find your clothing reeks of the smell of fuel.

"The first time I went out on the deck onto the flight deck during air operations, I was scared," Sean recalls. "I really was.

"I was being trained by two other guys, and we were underneath an F-4. I was supposed to be learning how to hook up a holdback.

"Because of the noise, you have to communicate with hand signals, and the guy in charge started signaling me. He was trying to tell me which way to run out from under the plane after we had finished the hookup.

"But I got mixed up, since it was the first time up there. I thought he was telling me, 'Go on, get out of here; we'll take care of it.' So I just dropped the cable and ran.

"Later, everyone kidded me about it."

Every man who works on the flight deck knows of at least one accident that has taken place during air operations. Sean tells about a catapult officer on the *Enterprise* who gave the pilot the wrong signal. The pilot revved up his engine before the holdback cable was in place. "The plane ran over the officer and three other guys," says Sean. "The officer was the only one that lived."

When there is an accident, it's usually caused by human error, human failure, Sean says. His job causes him no fear.

"It's exciting up on the deck," Sean says. "I know it's something I'll never experience again in my life.

"Take at night, for example. You go up onto the deck and there's no light at all; you can hardly see your hand in front of your face.

"Then a plane goes into afterburners [burning exhaust fumes to produce additional thrust], and suddenly the whole sky lights up.

Sean examines a tension bar on the quiet, planeless flight deck of the *Nimitz*.

"And you might be crouched down under the plane when it does that." Sean shakes his head and grins. "Well," he says, "it gives you a feeling you'll never forget."

In time, Sean was placed in charge of hooking up aircraft for launching, and assigned his post within the bubble. Men who work for him now do the actual hooking up.

Sean feels good about being in the Navy. "Sure, sometimes I think about it and wish I hadn't joined," he says, "but other times I look around, and see what I've got, and I know I wouldn't have it if it wasn't for the Navy.

"Like I just got a car, a brand-new Camaro. And I'm planning on getting married in the fall to my girlfriend back home.

"If I had stayed in White Hall, I'd probably be working on a farm or in a farm supply store. So everything has worked out all right. Everything's fine."

Charles Brown, twenty-five, a native of Jamaica, became a United States citizen while serving aboard the *Nimitz*. He was fifteen when his parents immigrated to the United States. They settled in Brooklyn, where Charles attended Samuel J. Tilden High School. Afterward, he went to Pratt Institute, also in Brooklyn, for a year.

"Then I got fed up with college," he says. "I decided I wanted something different, and that's when I joined the Navy."

When Charles first went aboard the *Nimitz,* he was assigned to the Deck Department. He did a great deal of scrubbing and mopping, and sweeping and painting. He didn't like that very much. Because he had always been interested in navigation, he sent for a correspondence course that would help to train him in the science of plotting and directing the ship's course. When he had completed the course, he requested and was granted a transfer to the ship's Navigation Department.

As a member of the Navigation Department, Charles was trained as a helmsman—that is, he sometimes steers the ship. He is, in fact, one of the four Master Helmsmen aboard the *Nimitz*.

When the *Nimitz* is steaming in open water, far from land or other vessels, a boatswain's mate from the Deck Department does the steering.

Charles Brown (right)—"The Navy really showed me that if I don't go back to school . . . my life is going to be difficult."

But either Charles or some other member of the Navigation Department does the steering when a delicate touch is required. For instance, Charles often mans the helm when the *Nimitz* is taking on fuel or supplies from another ship at sea. The two vessels must speed along side by side, always keeping exactly the same distance apart. A cool and experienced hand is needed at the helm at such times—which Charles supplies.

Anytime the *Nimitz* enters a harbor to anchor or dock, a Master Helmsman also takes over. The same holds true when the ship leaves a port.

The helm is located within the wheelhouse, the navigational control center of the ship. It's also called the bridge. Besides the helmsman, the officer on watch in charge of the ship—called the Officer of the Deck, the OOD—is posted there. And so is the quartermaster of the watch, who is in charge of the navigational equipment.

A lee helmsman, who stands just to Charles' right as he mans the wheel, operates the engine order telegraph, a signal system that transmits orders concerning the vessel's speed and direction from the OOD to the engine room.

Charles turns the wheel according to instruction given him by the Officer of the Deck. For example, the OOD may tell him to steer a course of 175 degrees. There's a compass mounted above and just forward of the wheel and Charles watches it constantly, easing the wheel a bit in one direction, then in the other, to maintain the proper heading. "Sometimes I have to maintain a heading to within one-quarter of a degree," Charles says. "It can be hairy."

The wheel that Charles turns, about the size of an automobile steering wheel, controls steering engines that are located in the ship's stern. The steering engines, in turn, move the ship's rudders.

Each rudder is a flat piece of steel that is suspended by a hinge system from the stern of the ship. When a rudder is turned to the right, water flowing by the ship exerts pressure against it. The pressure swings the stern to the left (thereby sending the bow of the ship to the right).

Another of Charles' duties is to maintain the deck log, which is a complete and detailed record of all that happens aboard the *Nimitz* from a standpoint of navigation. Whenever there's a change in the vessel's speed or heading, Charles must note it in the log. Weather conditions have to be logged, too. Charles calls the log a "chronological history of the ship." It began on the day the vessel went into operation, and will continue throughout the life of the ship.

Charles has mixed feelings about the trips he's made to foreign ports. A voyage to the Mediterranean thrilled him. "We went to the Holy Land," he says. "I never even dreamed I'd ever go there.

"I also got to see a lot of Europe, particularly Italy and Greece. I enjoyed that. We also went to Africa, to Tangiers [in Morocco]."

Charles was disappointed, however, that he didn't get to know the countries he visited. He felt that there was little opportunity to become involved with people, mostly because of the language barrier. "In the Navy," he says, "you really don't get to see a country; you only glimpse it."

Charles missed his girlfriend back home. And when he visited exotic places, he missed her more than ever. "I wanted her to be with me," he says, "to share my experiences."

While Charles feels his two-year stay aboard the *Nimitz* has been a "positive" experience for him, he has no interest in making a career of the Navy. He intends to return to college, to Pratt Institute, and study to be an architect.

Under the terms of his enlistment, the federal government will provide funds for Charles' education. "It'll be much easier for me to go to school now," he says. "I'll be able to concentrate more on learning, rather than having to spend time and effort earning money to pay for my education."

Charles feels the Navy helped to mature him. "I'm better motivated now," he says. "I'm older and, I hope, wiser.

"The Navy really showed me that if I don't go back to school and get an education, the rest of my life is going to be difficult."

8/

The Supercarriers, Pros and Cons

The *Nimitz* plows through choppy waters of the Indian Ocean, bound for the Persian Gulf, its flight deck the scene of frantic activity. One by one, and sometimes two by two, aircraft rip down the runways and lift into the air.

The *Nimitz,* along with the *Forrestal,* is operating as the cutting edge of the Sixth Fleet's Task Force 60, which also consists of cruisers, destroyers, and frigates that are escorting the carriers.

Intelligence reports have disclosed that a Soviet strike force, which includes land-based bombers, missile-firing submarines, cruisers, destroyers, and high-speed missile boats, is poised to cut off oil supplies headed for Europe and the United States.

Into the air go two F-14 Tomcats. Their Phoenix missile systems can shoot down Soviet jets and destroy the missiles they fire. The F-14s are followed by a single Hawkeye. Its radar can detect anything within a 250-mile radius, and the plane's computers can monitor up to 300 targets simultaneously and report their position, speed, and course to computers in the F-14s.

When a Hawkeye reports "multiple radar contacts inbound" to the intelligence control center aboard the *Nimitz,* the commander orders more F-14s into the air. Then, using his direct line to Navy headquarters

Nimitz steams along, accompanied by nuclear-powered *South Carolina* and *California*.

U.S.S. *Eisenhower*, following launching in 1975.

at the Pentagon in Washington, he requests permission for "weapon release" so that he can order his aircraft to fire before they are fired upon.

It's not the real thing, of course; it's war games, the method the Navy has traditionally used to keep its forces in a state of readiness.

The mission of the Sixth Fleet today is as challenging as any ever faced by an American naval force in peacetime. The Sixth Fleet "is responsible for the conduct of naval operations as may be directed by . . . national authorities . . . to insure control of the seas and air within the Mediterranean Sea, the Black Sea, in countries contiguous to or near the Mediterranean Sea."

To carry out its mission, the Sixth Fleet has 40 to 50 ships and approximately 200 aircraft which are divided into eight task forces. In the Pacific Ocean, the Seventh Fleet of comparable size, has similar responsibilities.

But the Navy's mission is getting more difficult all the time.

When World War II ended, the United States could boast the mightiest Navy the world had ever seen. The Soviet Union's Navy was feeble by comparison. The Soviets had only two large warships, both of which had been borrowed, one from the United States, the other from Great Britain. They had a few other small surface ships. Their submarine fleet was of good size, but aging.

In the years that the United States was preoccupied with Vietnam, the Soviets began developing a global Navy that has come to rival and even surpass that of the United States in size and weaponry. In terms of number of vessels, this is how the two nations compared at the beginning of the 1980s, according to Department of Defense statistics:

	SOVIET UNION	UNITED STATES
Aircraft Carriers	2	12
Cruisers	37	27
Destroyers/Frigates	195	129
Attack submarines	260	77
Nuclear-missile submarines	91	41
Other ships	397	172

Soviet reconnaissance vessel crosses bow of *Nimitz* in Virginia coastal waters.

Today, the Soviet Union operates freely in all of the world's oceans. The first Soviet ship was assigned to the eastern Mediterranean in 1964. The number of Russian vessels operating there by 1979 had grown to about 50.

Soviet surface ships have been operating off the West Coast of Africa since 1970. In the Indian Ocean they now maintain a force of from 18 to 20 ships.

In 1979, the Soviet Union reportedly sent 89 submarines into the Atlantic Ocean as part of a huge training exercise. Twice that same year, Soviet warships were spotted in the Gulf of Mexico, not far from New Orleans.

Soviet reconnaissance vessels seem to be everywhere. When a Navy warship leaves an American port, it frequently comes under the scrutiny of a Russian vessel as soon as it enters international waters. Such vessels are sometimes registered as fishing trawlers, but they bristle with many types of radar gear and antenna, used for locating and listening.

United States strategists agree that a potentially hostile power should not be permitted to dominate the seas. The Navy's answer to the situation is, to a great extent, based upon the supercarrier.

As a military weapon, the supercarrier is unique for several reasons.

First, it provides air power at sea. In order to gain control of the seas, it's first necessary to gain control of the air above the seas. The carrier provides the aircraft to achieve this superiority.

Second, the carrier provides mobility. It can cruise the oceans of the world, which make up three-quarters of the earth's surface, without the necessity of political negotiation. When it's needed, the carrier simply pulls up anchor and heads for the trouble spot.

Third, the carrier offers *complete* support. It is, after all, a floating air base, with aircraft and their weaponry, their bombs and missiles. It carries the pilots to fly the planes and the mechanics and shops to service them. It carries jet fuel. The minute the carrier arrives at a trouble spot, it's ready.

Fourth, a carrier is flexible, with the ability to carry out a wide range of assignments. It can be used merely to demonstrate the nation's presence or it can serve in any type of military confrontation or limited war. It can also play a role, say carrier enthusiasts, in a nuclear conflict.

At the beginning of the 1980s, the Navy had 12 supercarriers in operation. They were of four different classes:

Combat information center aboard the *Nimitz*.

THE SUPERCARRIERS

Name	Number	Year Completed	Displacement (Tons)	Length of Flight Deck (Feet)
United States	CV-58	(Cancelled)	—	—
Forrestal	CV-59	1955	79,250	1,039
Saratoga	CV-60	1956	80,000	1,039
Ranger	CV-61	1957	80,000	1,046
Independence	CV-62	1959	80,000	1,046
Kitty Hawk	CV-63	1961	80,300	1,047
Constellation	CV-64	1961	80,300	1,047
Enterprise	CVN-65	1961	85,000	1,040
America	CV-66	1965	81,700	1,047
John F. Kennedy	CV-67	1968	80,000	1,051
Nimitz	CVN-68	1975	91,000	1,092
Dwight D. Eisenhower	CVN-69	1980	91,000	1,092
Carl Vinson	CVN-70	1981 (est.)	91,000	1,092

• *Nimitz* class—The *Nimitz* (CVN-68), a 91,000-ton vessel, was commissioned in May, 1975, the first of a three-ship class of nuclear-powered carriers. The others are the *Dwight D. Eisenhower* (CVN-69) and the *Carl Vinson* (CVN-70).

• The *Enterprise* (CVN-65)—The first nuclear-powered carrier, 85,000 tons, commissioned in 1961.

• *Forrestal* class—The 79,250-ton *Forrestal* (CV-59) went into service in 1955. Including the *Forrestal*, there are eight ships in this class. The others are the *Saratoga* (CV-60), *Ranger* (CV-61), *Independence* (CV-62), *Kitty Hawk* (CV-63), *Constellation* (CV-64), *America* (CV-66), and *John F. Kennedy* (CV-67).

In addition to these 12 ships, there were two other aircraft carriers in operation in 1980, the *Midway*

(CV-41) and the *Coral Sea* (CV-43). Both of these vessels were scheduled to be withdrawn from service in the early 1980s.

Supercarriers have their critics. Some military experts say that the carrier is no longer essential for providing air cover for the fleet or projecting firepower against enemy ships or land bases. In these instances, the carrier's role has been displaced by land-based missiles and missile-launching submarines.

Supercarriers are also criticized for their basic defensive shortcomings, their vulnerability. Consider that a carrier on active duty is laden down with bombs, missiles, and rockets. There's the superheated steam of the catapults and the fiery exhaust of jet aircraft. There's liquid oxygen aboard and acres and acres of painted surfaces. There are thousands of gallons of jet fuel. And on nonnuclear vessels, there is the black fuel oil that such ships burn.

Someone once described the modern carrier as "a floating bomb." Many people believe that description to be close to the truth.

Since a carrier's defense is based on its fighters, anything that prevents those aircraft from being launched has to endow the ship with a "sitting duck" status. Suppose the catapults are damaged and have to shut down. "Without those catapults, we're no longer a fighting ship," says one carrier officer. "We're just a big hotel."

Those who support carriers say that they are harder to sink than any other ship afloat. They can shake off torpedoes, missiles, and even near misses with nuclear weapons and keep right on operating.

In mid-January, 1969, when the carrier *Enterprise* was cruising peacefully during training exercises not far from Pearl Harbor, a series of thunderous explosions suddenly rocked the ship, and fires raged out of control.

Fire teams quickly swung into action, preventing the flames from reaching the ship's nuclear reactors. Captain Kent L. Lee turned the *Enterprise* into the wind in an effort to fan the flames off the ship's stern. It took four hours to quench the fire.

Afterward, the *Enterprise* looked like the victim of a bombing attack. Cables dangled loosely from the ship's side and big steel plates were blackened and buckled. Holes as large as 20 feet in diameter were ripped in the ship's flight deck. Some radio antennas were knocked out.

Air operations aboard the *Nimitz* as viewed from bridge.

Primary control center on board the *Nimitz* during flight operations.

The fiery explosions left 25 sailors dead. Scores were injured.

But, today, looking back, the Navy cites the tragic accident as a demonstration of the modern carrier's defensive strength.

An investigation of the accident revealed that nine big-caliber bombs had accidentally been detonated on the flight deck of the *Enterprise*. This was calculated as an explosive force equal to that of six antiship missiles. It took weeks to repair the damage. Yet the *Enterprise* could have remained in operation. "Despite the major damage to the flight deck," a Navy spokeman says, "all essential systems in the ship were maintained in operational status.

"Effective damage control contained the effects of the fire. The ship could have resumed scheduled air operations within a matter of hours, as soon as the debris was cleared from the flight deck."

Carriers built during the 1970s and 1980s have even greater defensive strength than the *Enterprise*, says the Navy. Flight decks and lower decks are armored with steel of special strength. Bombs, rockets, missiles, and aviation fuel are stored in heavily armored compartments.

An energy-absorbing hull design is meant to counter the explosive warhead of big-caliber torpedoes. Carrier interiors are constructed in honeycomb fashion, with more than 2,000 watertight and shock-resistant compartments to limit damage and flooding.

For protection against fire, *Nimitz*-class carriers are divided into fire zones by 10 evenly spaced steel bulkheads that run crosswise in the ship. Smoke and flames can be isolated within one zone by securing

Passageways aboard the *Nimitz* are several city blocks in length.

hatches in the bulkheads. Alarm systems that respond to smoke and heat have been installed throughout the ship wherever high temperatures would be hazardous.

Fire mains (similar to those on city streets), sprinkler systems, and flight deck washdown systems are also available for fighting fires.

Burning liquid, such as aviation fuel, cannot be extinguished with water. A foam substance that smothers the flames must be used. *Nimitz*-class carriers offer a number of foam stations on the flight deck and hangar deck. In addition, there are small four-wheeled vehicles that can carry foam to any spot on the flight deck.

"We have drills every day," says one carrier captain. "Crews are continually being trained and retrained."

Then there are backup systems. "The Navy is a big believer in having alternate or substitute means of doing the same thing," says a carrier crewman.

For example, carriers have more than one command station, each capable of operating independently of the other. Should one station be knocked out by enemy attack, the ship can be controlled and commanded from the other.

On *Nimitz*-class carriers, there are four independent engines, several independent diesel generators, and four separate propellers.

Still, even the most enthusiastic of carrier supporters do not claim any carrier to be invulnerable to attack. But they hasten to add that "no weapon system, no individual unit, is invulnerable."

Some military experts say that land bases are superior to and should be used instead of aircraft carriers. After all, you can't "sink" a land base. But land bases are less than perfect. For instance, when the Korean War erupted in 1950, all available land bases were overrun by the North Korean army in the first day of action. Aircraft carriers were able to move in and provide immediate support.

There can also be a problem in supplying a land base. Long pipelines have had to be constructed to supply aviation fuel to the air bases the United States maintains in Spain. Such facilities provide tempting

Bow view of *Eisenhower* as vessel churns waters off Virginia coast.

targets for sabotage or terrorist attack, and thus must be constantly protected.

But the biggest problem has to do with the right to operate such bases. Permission has to be granted by the host country. Fewer and fewer nations are willing to grant such permission.

At the time the Korean War ended, the United States had more than 500 bases in foreign countries. By 1957, that number had been reduced to 100. By 1980, the number of overseas bases being used by United States aircraft had shrunk to 50.

Sometimes a change in government will result in the United States being ousted from an air base. Wheelus Air Base in Libya, the last of several bases the United States once utilized in North Africa, was closed to the United States in 1969 after Colonel Muammar el-Quaddafi came to power. Iran is another example. After the Shah of Iran was overthrown in 1978, the United States had to withdraw from bases in that country.

There is no substitute for the aircraft carrier, says the Navy, and argues that 12 carriers is the absolute minimum required in order to be able to meet its peacetime commitments.

Even though the Navy may have 12 carriers in operation, that does not mean it has 12 carriers available for use in foreign waters. At any given time, about one-third of the Navy's carrier force is in shipyards undergoing repair work or modernization. Another third is involved in training exercises, usually conducted in waters near the United States.

Thus, if there are 12 carriers in active service, only four are available for overseas assignment.

The Navy estimates a carrier's life expectancy to be about 30 years. Beginning in the mid-1980s, the eight carriers of the *Forrestal*-class, the first of which is the *Forrestal* itself, will begin reaching the end of their 30-year service lives.

Instead of replacing these vessels with new ships, the Navy is planning to overhaul them, one by one. New electric generators, electronic gear, and piping will be installed. Worn boiler parts and auxiliary machinery are to be replaced.

The Navy is hoping that its modernization program will extend the life of these ships by 15 years, from

Forrestal-class carriers, such as the *Ranger*, are scheduled for overhaul as part of Navy modernization program.

Keel-laying ceremonies for U.S.S.
Vinson **coincided with launching**
of ***Eisenhower.***

Artist's conception of the U.S.S. *Vinson* (CV-70), newest of the Navy's supercarriers.

30 to 45 years, and that the *Forrestal*-class ships will still be in service as the year 2000 approaches.

Most Navy strategists would like to see all new carriers be nuclear-propelled. The big advantage of a nuclear-powered ship is its ability to steam at high speed for an unlimited distance without refueling. In addition, because the nuclear carrier does not have to carry vast stores of its own fuel, more space can be given over to aviation fuel and other combat supplies.

Another argument for nuclear power is probably best typified by the No Gas signs that were displayed in service stations in every part of the United States in 1973 and beginning again in 1979. Supplies of petroleum from Persian Gulf countries are erratic at best. And with fuel shortages come higher and higher prices. As the cost of fossil fuels keep climbing, nuclear power becomes a better bargain.

But nuclear carriers are expensive to build, and they are getting more and more expensive all the time. The nuclear-powered *Enterprise,* constructed during the period from 1958 through 1961, cost approximately $450 million. Were the Navy to order another nuclear carrier today, one of the *Nimitz* class, the price tag would be close to $2.5 billion.

In 1979, President Jimmy Carter turned thumbs down on the Navy's request to build a fourth carrier of the *Nimitz* class. Instead, the President favored a smaller carrier, about two-thirds the size of the *Nimitz.* It would not be nuclear-powered.

Admiral Hyman G. Rickover, Director of the Navy's Nuclear Propulsion Program, said that such a compromise made no sense. He called the nuclear carrier "overwhelmingly superior" to other carriers proposed, on the basis of cost or any basis. To build an oil-fired ship in the 1980s, said Admiral Rickover, would be setting back the clock of nuclear technology by 15 to 30 years.

Later, President Carter changed course, saying that he favored a large nuclear-powered carrier. Congress had already approved such a vessel.

One thing is certain: Supercarriers are here to stay. They are not headed the way of the battleship, into extinction—not in this century, at least.

Will supercarriers of the future be the size of the *Nimitz* or will they be smaller, of *Forrestal* size?

Will they be oil-fired or nuclear-powered?

These are questions that will be answered in the years ahead.

But the nation's leaders agree that supercarriers are indispensable. They will dominate the Navy's thinking and strategy for decades to come.

Glossary

AFT—In, near, or toward a ship's stern.

AFTERBURNING—Combustion that results from the injection of fuel into the exhaust gases of a jet engine to produce additional thrust.

AMIDSHIPS—In the middle of a ship, along the line of the keel.

ASW—Abbreviation for antisubmarine warfare.

AVIONICS—The science and technology of electrical and electronic devices used in aviation.

BEAM—The extreme width of a ship.

BERTH—Space assigned a vessel for anchoring or mooring.

BRIDGE—The raised platform within the wheelhouse from which a ship is steered and navigated.

BRIDLE—In launching an airplane, the metal strap that connects the plane to the shuttle.

BOAT—A small open or decked-over craft propelled by oars, sails, or some type of engine; also, any vessel carried aboard a larger vessel for its use.

BOATSWAIN—A petty officer in charge of deck work.

BOOT CAMP—Slang for naval recruit training center (where recruits must wear "boots," or leggings).

BOOTS—Slang for leggings worn by naval recruits.

BORE—The interior of a gun barrel.

BOW—The forward section of a vessel.

BULKHEAD—The wall of a room aboard a ship, or any wall-like surface.

BUNK—A built-in bed aboard a ship.

BUOY—A floating marker anchored to the bottom, which by shape or color imparts navigational information.

CAT—Short for catapult.

CATAPULT—The mechanism used for launching aircraft aboard an aircraft carrier.

COMMISSION—To activate a ship or aircraft.

COMPARTMENT—Space enclosed by bulkheads, a deck, and overhead, corresponding to a room in a building.

DECK—Any surface on a ship that corresponds to the floor of a building on land.

DECKHAND—A seaman assigned to the Deck Department.

DECOMMISSION—To withdraw a ship from active service.

DISPLACEMENT—The amount of water a ship displaces expressed in displacement tons.

DISPLACEMENT TON—A unit for measuring the displacement of a ship, equal to 2,240 pounds.

DOSIMETER—A device carried on a person for measuring the quantity of radiation to which he has been exposed.

DRAFT—The depth to which a vessel is immersed, as measured from water's surface to the vessel's keel.

ENGINE ORDER TELEGRAPH—A signaling device that transmits speed directions from the Officer of the Deck to the engine room.

FLIGHT DECK—The deck of an aircraft carrier on which the planes take off and land.

FORWARD—Toward the bow; opposite of aft.

FRAME—One of the many metal ribs of a ship.

FUNNEL—A ship's smokestack; stack.

GUIDED MISSILE—An aerial missile, such as a rocket, steered by radio signals or other electronic controls.

HANGAR DECK—On an aircraft carrier, the enclosed deck just below the flight deck where airplanes are stored, maintained, and repaired.

HATCH—An opening in a ship's bulkhead or deck; a door or doorway.

HAWSEPIPE—A metal-lined opening in the bow of a ship through which the anchor chain passes.

HELM—The wheel by which the ship is steered.

HELMSMAN—The person who steers the ship.

HOLD—A space below decks meant for storage.

HOLDBACK—The metal cable that prevents an aircraft from surging forward just before it is catapulted from the deck.

HULL—The framework of a vessel, including plating and decks.

IN MOTHBALLS—To be put in storage; to be inactivated.

ISLAND—The superstructure of an aircraft carrier.

JEEP CARRIER—See Merchant Aircraft Carrier.

KEEL—The central fore-to-aft structural part of a ship.

KNOT—A unit of speed equal to one nautical mile (approximately 1.15 statute miles) per hour.

LADDER—On a ship, a structure that corresponds to a flight of stairs in a building.

LANDING SAFETY OFFICER—The officer in charge of directing an aircraft as it approaches and lands on a carrier deck.

LEAVE—Authorized absence from a ship or shore base.

LEE HELMSMAN—An assistant helmsman, often assigned to control the engine order telegraph.

LIBERTY—Shore leave; a period of authorized absence from a ship or shore station, usually less than 48 hours.

LOG—A record of the ship's operation.

LSO—Abbreviation for Landing Safety Officer.

MEATBALL—Slang for the reflected beam of light as seen in the mirror of the mirror landing system.

MERCHANT AIRCRAFT CARRIER—A type of carrier used as an escort vessel and to support landing operations during World War II. Also called "jeep carrier." Merchant Aircraft Carriers were converted cargo vessels or tankers.

MESS HALL—The place where shipboard personnel eat; a dining hall.

MESSMAN—An enlisted man who serves in the mess hall.

MIRROR LANDING SYSTEM—A method used to aid pilots in carrier landings. The system is based on a reflected beam of light which produces an optical glide path that the incoming pilot follows to the flight deck.

NAUTICAL MILE—A distance of 6,080.2 feet, or about one-sixth more than a land mile.

OFFICER OF THE DECK—The officer on watch in charge of the ship.

OOD—Abbreviation for Officer of the Deck.

OVERHEAD—The ceiling of a room aboard ship, or any ceiling-like surface.

PACK—A cluster of aircraft parked on the carrier deck.

PILOTHOUSE—See Wheelhouse.

PORT—The left side of a ship when a person is facing forward.

QUARTERMASTER—An individual charged with the navigation of a ship.

RADAR—A method of determining the location of an object by measuring the speed and direction of reflected radio waves.

RANK—The grade or official standing of an officer.

RATE—The grade or official standing of an enlisted man.

RATING—One's Navy occupation, as storekeeper, machinist's mate, sonarman, etc.

READY ROOM—A room in which pilots and other air crew members receive orders before takeoff.

RUDDER—The vertical blade mounted at the stern of the ship beneath the water, used in changing the ship's direction.

SAM—An acronym for surface-to-air missile.

SEAPLANE—An aircraft equipped with floats that can take off from either land or water.

SHIP—Any large ocean-going craft.

SHUTTLE—The device that moves back and forth in a slot of the flight deck of an aircraft carrier, and to which the plane is attached for launching.

SONAR—A method of detecting and locating submerged objects by analyzing reflected sound waves.

STACK—Short for smokestack.

STARBOARD—The right side of a ship when a person is facing forward.

STERN—The back or rear of a vessel.

SUPERSTRUCTURE—All of the ship's equipment and fittings above the hull, excepting armament.

TENDER—A ship used to attend other vessels or aircraft, as a seaplane tender.

U.S.S.—Abbreviation for United States Ship.

WATCH—A period of duty, usually of four hours' duration.

WATERLINE—The line at which the water's surface borders a ship.

WHEELHOUSE—The compartment within the superstructure wherein the OOD, helmsman, and quartermaster of the watch stand their watches; also called a pilothouse.

WINDLASS—A device for hoisting that resembles a horizontal drum to which rope or cable is attached.

Index